Everybody Needs a Screw

What I learned from selling
fasteners for forty years

Steven Yates

authorHOUSE®

AuthorHouse™
1663 Liberty Drive
Bloomington, IN 47403
www.authorhouse.com
Phone: 833-262-8899

Published by AuthorHouse 05/24/2022

ISBN: 978-1-6655-5961-4 (sc)
ISBN: 978-1-6655-5960-7 (hc)
ISBN: 978-1-6655-5959-1 (e)

Print information available on the last page.

CONTENTS

PREFACE

For the past forty years, I have been hacking around the fastener industry. I have met some pretty interesting people; many of them are (or were) real characters. I have seen some pretty weird things happen. This book presents the best of these characters and describes many of these experiences. When I started writing this book a long, long time ago, I used the real names of people and real names of companies. I sent a copy of it to a very dear friend, who told me he laughed out loud. I sent one to a sales rep who worked for me and had years and years of experience; he suggested I might get sued. I told him I would change the names of people and their companies if I ever to attempted to publish it. I did.

I had to change them all. The stories and events are all factual, but all the names of people and their companies have been changed. Some of these companies don't exist anymore, and many of the unnamed people are no longer with us. This is part of the reason I wrote it. Many of them were wonderful people and should be remembered, even under pseudonyms.

INTRODUCTION

Don't we all need a screw? Everybody needs a good screw sometime. Everybody needs a screw at one time or another. No, you dirty-minded people, I don't mean *that* kind of screw. I'm talking about the kind that holds things together.

Nearly every company in the world that actually manufactures something needs screws or some sort of fasteners to hold their product together. Every household in the world needs screws, nuts, bolts, and washers, as well as all sorts of small parts that fall under the very general term of "fasteners." Whenever us folks in the industry mention that we are in the fastener business, we are often asked if that is zippers or buttons. And when we say we are in the screw business, things can get confusing.

Where households are concerned, they are usually kept in coffee cans. Why? You never know when you are going to need one. They will just lay there and get rusty. When the need arises, you will not have the one you need. So off you go to the local Ace Hardware, Home Depot, or Lowe's to spend from ten to fifteen cents for the one you need. Not really so much money. If you include your gas and time, it's still not so much money really and only a minor inconvenience. After all, it's only a few pennies, right?

Way back when I was a little kid, growing up in central Iowa, I played sandlot baseball and football, swam, and fished; everyone, even people in the Bible Belt, needed screws. Heck, my dad bought screws all the time, but he didn't just buy the kind you keep in a can or jar. For forty years, he was a purchasing agent and bought many products, including screws, nuts, and bolts.

Most men (I don't mean to slight women) keep them all jumbled up; for some unknown reason, they think they'll use them sometime in the future. All mixed up, half of them rusty, and none of them of any use whatsoever and will never be used, but it is important to keep them. You never know when we might need one of them. I have quarter kegs that weight fifty pounds each full of all sizes and types of them and will likely never use any of them. They are worthless. Because I, like most men, never have the one I need; we all make that trip to buy the one we need. We usually buy more than we need and throw the rest into the same coffee can, knowing that we will never remember what they went to, but not so my dad. There are anal-retentive people, and then there was my father. His garage was not only neat, it was perfect. Every tool was hanging on a peg board where he could put his hands on it, and every nut, bolt, screw, or washer was not only sorted by product but labeled in separate little drawers by size. Did this ensure him having what he needed? Hell no, and it drove him nuts, or should I say crazy. He had all the nuts except, of course, the one he needed.

Why does this age-old process especially upset a person who has been selling them for some forty years? Easy: Fastener people like us know what the damn things cost to make.

Do the math. Fifteen cents should be no big deal, right? It's only a dime and a nickel. What's all the fuss about? Well, let's take, for example, a 10-24 × ½ slotted round head steel machine zinc-plated screw. This is a pretty common part. If you want one from the local hardware store, it may cost you fifteen or twenty cents. Hey, that's pretty cheap, isn't it? We fastener people know that if you wanted to buy one thousand of them, they would weigh about five pounds. So, we refer to that as five pounds per thousand. You see, when you are in the fastener industry, we sell them by the thousand, not one at a time.

Screws are made out of wire, huge coils of steel wire that are chopped up and cold formed into the shape of a screw. They are then thread rolled. Threads used to be cut on a lathe one at a time. Early in the twentieth century, folks in the business invented faster and more efficient ways to form screws and bolts. (Sorry, I'm getting sidetracked; I'll get into the actually manufacturing process later.) The cold heading wire used to make screws may cost as much as eighty cents a pound. This means that one thousand of our parts cost four dollars per thousand in raw material. Again, I will get into the technical end a little later, but basically, the total cost of this little screw would be seven or eight dollars per thousand.

So now being a good salesman, you try to sell this little screw for around eleven or twelve dollars per thousand. Now to throw a wrench into this plan, these particular parts are rarely made in the United States today. It's too standard. They are imported by the million and sold to the fastener people for half that price. Oops, now we have a price of $5.50 per thousand. Now, what do we pay our local hardware store again? That fifteen-cent screw is actually costing you … I'll wait for you to get out your calculator; that's right: $150 per thousand. When you are in the fastener industry and know that the cost of that screw is actually half a penny each, and you have to pay fifteen cents each, it's maddening.

I mentioned that my father worked in the Purchasing Department. He started shortly before World War II broke out. After Pearl Harbor was attacked, he thought he would join the Navy and become a cook. He loved to cook and thought this would be a good way for him to serve his country. But he was drafted into the Army before he could join the Navy and spent three years in the Pacific. He returned home and spent the next forty years purchasing various products, one of which was fasteners.

Salesmen (women got into sales much later) called on my dad all the time. At a very young age, I was exposed to the fastener industry, and I grew up hearing the names of the companies and salespeople my dad especially liked. On a few occasions, our family was invited to go out for dinner with one of them. The one I remember most was the owner of one of the finest fastener manufacturers in the United States. When it went under, there were a number of very good companies that were started by the talented salespeople who had worked there.

As for myself, I grew up in the midst of the Bible Belt. My father and my mother, who was a schoolteacher in the public school system, provided a wonderful home life for us. Central Iowa was deep in the Bible Belt, and the 1950s and 1960s were very prosperous. That was a very innocent time in our country. My brother and I had a wonderful childhood. He was three years older than me and was not only an artist, but an architecture graduate. Tragically, he was killed in a one-car accident in 1967. The following June, I was married. We moved to our college town, where I earned a double major in history and physical education. I was equipped to teach and coach. I knew the difference between a nut and a screw. That was the extent of my fastener knowledge.

To anyone familiar with the early 1970s, there was an absolute glut of schoolteachers. There were so many of us in the market, that if a position opened in a good school system, there would be literally hundreds of applicants. We were a dime a dozen. I was very fortunate to get a job at a small Catholic school in central Iowa.

Relax. I know this has nothing to do with screws, but you should know how polluted my life became because of screws. I was the first non-Catholic lay teacher they ever hired. Maybe that's why I had such a wonderful experience for two years. The school had very little money, and there was no future there, but I loved it. The kids were a delight, and the administration was wonderful. I had to look at this as a stepping-stone to something else. I resigned and started looking for a better position. There weren't many teaching positions available. I was either underqualified for what a school wanted, which I could grudgingly agree with, or I was told I was way overqualified, which completely puzzled me. Regardless, as I saw it, there was no future in the education business.

In the summer of 1972, I took a job at a local slaughterhouse. They didn't process the meat there; they aged it and then shipped it to places like Madison, Wisconsin; Dubuque, Iowa; Los Angeles, and Chicago, where the hot dogs and chopped ham was processed. They paid very well, but I had to do some of the worst things a human should have to do. The plant slaughtered up to six thousand hogs a day. The processing of them is not a pretty picture.

Summer turned into fall, and no teaching jobs came up. I was thinking of entering the company's management training program. They had pretty good benefits, and I was thinking I might make a life for myself killing pigs. This was when I made the first of many huge mistakes that led me to the screw business.

Life takes many turns, and we all come to crossroads. It is amazing how different our lives would have been if we had made different decisions at these times. The placement office at the university called me and got me an interview at a school on Chicago's North Shore.

I didn't know anything about this area, only that it was a suburb of Chicago. Jan, my lovely wife, and I were flown into Chicago, where I was interviewed and then hired. This was one of my biggest mistakes. If you don't know this area, the North Shore has one of the highest per capita incomes in the United States. I taught and coached there for only one year. It was a terrible experience, but a good learning one. I learned how messed up really rich people can be. For instance, there were two boys, in fifth and seventh grades, living by themselves in a twenty-six-room mansion. Their parents, both surgeons, were divorced and travelled a lot. They had a live-in nurse or housekeeper who was never there. Like the movie *Home Alone*, they lived like animals, and the house was a disaster. The other residents of that community were either old money or new money. These are the ones who live in a mansion but have hot dogs in the fridge.

In review, we had moved from a lively college town to a very small community. We grew to love it. Everyone knew everyone, and we were treated so nice. Now in the big city we didn't know anyone and became very lonely. The upper crust of upper crust of the North Shore was not a good fit. I again resigned. We had no jobs and no real prospects. It was June of 1973, and I was beginning to wonder what I was going to do with my life. I had turned my back on what seemed to be a good chance at a management position in a big firm, and now nine months later, I was stuck in Chicago with no future. There were no teaching or coaching jobs available. I had no training to do anything else. I was considering going back to school to get a master's degree; after all, we didn't have any children yet, and it would only take another year.

CHAPTER 1

HOW IT ALL BEGAN

Then one evening in early June, another one of those crossroad events occurred. I got a phone call from a gentleman who was the owner of a small fastener company. I had heard his name mentioned by my father but had forgotten who he was. He told me he had sold fasteners to Dad for many, many years, both as a salesman and now via the company he owned. He said he was talking to my father, who told him about my situation. He then asked if I was interested in coming over for an interview. In all honesty, I was not really flattered.

My thought pattern went this way: Was he trying to hire me as a hook? I didn't think this was a good idea. It could backfire on him, if it didn't work out.

I said, "I am honored, but honestly, I don't know anything about business, sales, or fasteners. All I know is how to teach school and coach sports."

He then said to me, "You sound just like your dad. He is one of the most honest men I have ever dealt with. He is a no-nonsense, straightforward man, and if you are a product of him, and sounds like you are, I would like to meet you."

Holy crap. What a statement. As I said earlier, I knew that Dad was a neat freak, very religious, and very principled, a retired Army major. He did his best to instill those principles in my brother and me. His other philosophy was to give an employer eight hours of work for eight hours of pay.

But he added, "You are going to be spending at least one-third of your life on a job. Make sure you enjoy what you are doing because life is too short and too precious to waste doing something you hate."

This is good advice for anyone. I had no idea how well it would serve me in the years to come;.

Well, of course, I had to go and meet him. He offered me a job. That was how it all began. My journey had begun. The people in this goofy industry have an old saying: Once you start, you can't get out of it; it's like a death sentence. It's true. It is like a death sentence.

Fortunately (or unfortunately), there is another saying that is true: "There is no such thing as job security in this industry, but if you are good, there is security within the industry." This means that if you are good and know the industry, you'll always be able to find work. There are employers that don't feel any shred of loyalty to their employees but expect total devotion. Some really only want to use you. You are expected to give your soul to them. But if you are good, there is always security within the industry. I don't know if this is true in other businesses, but it is in this one. If you are good, there is always someone that will pay for your abilities. Some companies will actually ask you how much business you can bring to them. "Do you have a following?" Whenever this was asked of me, and it often was, I would say, "I honestly cannot promise anything but my abilities to either purchase or sell your product." There were some who didn't offer me a job without that promise. I was also happy not to work under that sort of pressure.

I am almost never going to be serious in the following pages. But I have a serious reason for writing it. We old-timers always say to ourselves that the business is not what it used to be. That it used to be fun. These are not just the rantings and ravings of a bunch of old farts. It is a fact. Today, business is so impersonal, what with emails, Twitter, voicemail, and computer readouts. Business is not conducted the way it used to be.

Today, you can't make what is known as a cold call. Every personal sales contact has to be made by appointment only. To get one, you have to call the purchasing agent. But you usually only get voice mail. So, you leave a message, and they don't return your call. If you go to the company in person, they often don't even have a receptionist. I've made a sales call where the company had an empty lobby No one was in the lobby, only a lonely telephone and a list of extensions. When you call the appropriate one, guess what? That's right: voice mail.

Quotations are sent out via the internet or something called open-marked bidding, where orders are awarded to the cheapest bidder. Or a quote is sent out on a computer disc. Orders are sent out via EDI or email. No one has to speak personally to anyone else. (Oops, here comes the old fogey in me again.) You have purchasing people who have no idea what they are buying; they don't know where the parts are used, what the application is, or if they are appropriate for the function they are intended for, and they don't care. That's someone else's responsibility. Communications skills are a thing of the past.

The owner of a company I worked for said that sales are closed and future business is made through personalities. At one time, he was right. The talents of the salesperson provided buyers with trust. That is gone with the advent of this impersonal way of doing business.

The saddest part of this is that we now have salespeople who have no idea what they are selling or if they are the right parts for how the customer intends to use them. Engineers often think they know everything. The fact is, they are probably not fastener experts. A good salesperson who knows the business can (and should) recommend the right part for an application. So now, in many cases, we have the blind leading the blind. The word no is not in the vocabulary of some vendors.

Believe me when I say this causes a lot of problems for all parties involved. The good working relationships that went on for years between vendor and customer, where trust was a huge part of the relationship, are gone. Bean counters control which vendors supply parts, and that results in quality problems down the road. And the pressure from foreign sources and the cost of labor has forced a lot more manufacturing to move outside the United States, to China or India or somewhere else. This reduced the manufacturing base in our country and subsequently the fastener business. There have been some huge changes in the business world. Personal touch and communication skills are a thing of the past. The times I am going to tell you about are gone, but hopefully not forever.

So here we go. It is June of 1973. I knew nothing about business or fasteners or purchasing or inventory or manufacturing or sales, or, well, anything except how to coach basketball and teach history, which I was afraid was not going to serve me very well in the business world.

CHAPTER 2

THE TRAINING

I was no longer coaching basketball, swimming, track, football, and girls fast-pitch softball, nor teaching one of the social studies, my favorite being history. I was going to work for a fastener manufacturer that made screws and distributed nuts, bolts, and everything else that falls under the umbrella term "fastener." I really knew nothing about business, manufacturing, purchasing, inventory control; hell, I only got a C in economics. My instructor was really neat and tried to make an otherwise painfully boring subject interesting, but she was never able to get me very interested in it, and besides, that was a long time ago and long forgotten. But there was no way, I figured, that I would be able to relate any of that yearlong class to what I was now doing. Boy, was I correct, there is nothing that makes any sense in this business. I don't know about any other businesses, but this one is really strange. I thought that nothing in that class could apply to what I would be asked to do in this adventure. I was wrong again.

On my very first day, Charlie, the president of the company sat me down in his office and gave me a large blue book titled *Fastener Standards*, fifth edition. Most industries have a set of standards they use. Very wisely, he told me not to try to read it but to become familiar with it, to learn how to use it as a reference book. He called it the bible of the industry, and he was correct. He told me he eventually wanted me in the Sales Department, but before he'd have me sell anything, he wanted me to know every facet of the business. While not the best manager of people, he was still pretty wise in how he handled me as a greenhorn. He was a good businessman. He owned a successful company and treated his employees fairly.His only fault was that he was also quick to anger; sometimes, he would go absolutely nuts. As long as he stayed in his office, watching the stock market returns, reviewing profit and loss reports, and making plans for his next golf game or Las Vegas trip, and allowed us to do our jobs, everything was relatively quiet. But if we were shorthanded somewhere and he decided to leave his office and get involved, all hell could erupt.

He started my education by putting me in the warehouse to work with a completely psychotic human being. The company was family owned, and the warehouse manager was the president's father. James was even more volatile than his son. I was not asked to dump or repack screws. I was not told to drive a forklift truck or to unload a truck or to put parts in or take them out of inventory, all of which are warehouse jobs. I was told only to observe and learn the traffic of parts.

Finished parts from the factory were in the back of the building and came up front to the warehouse. From there, the parts were sent to other companies to have the oil cleaned off, to be heat-treated for hardening, or to be plated with any number of finishes. The warehouse manager's job was to coordinate and keep track of the traffic of all the parts and to get them shipped on time to the customer. It is a high-pressure job. He used four-letter words between every other word as loud as he could yell them. Truth be known, he had a heart of gold but, I guess he thought that profanity was the best way of getting things done.

Not everything we sold was made in our factory. Like all fastener manufacturers, we made only a narrow range of parts, but we also functioned as a distributor of parts purchased from other companies for our customers. Combining manufacturing and distribution requires good recordkeeping and a good sense of timing. The original equipment manufacturer (OEM) buys manufactured parts as well as distributed parts from the same supplier, so they can condense shipping and billing, not to mention that it's so very cheap compared to the cost of their product, but so very essential.

As I mentioned earlier, I grew up in the Bible Belt. My father never used obscenities, at least never in my presence. I was not completely protected from extreme vulgarity; I had heard those words before. Hell, I even used them myself from time to time, being careful not to say them where my parents might hear. I used some of them when I coached, but only for effect and never in anger. But the warehouse manager wove a tapestry of profanity that left a blue cloud hanging over the warehouse office from morning till night. It made no difference if he was on the telephone with one of our many suppliers or speaking with one of the company employees. He was really a very nice guy. He was thoughtful and very nice to me. But the string of swear words that spewed out of his mouth at other employees, truck drivers, and the folks he dealt with at the companies that did our heat-treating or plating was astonishing. He was a little guy, and the only reason no one challenged him or just plain kicked the crap out of him was that his son owned the company.

The other thing I was required to do in the warehouse was to pick up samples of everything. I pulled samples of everything that passed through the warehouse, whether it came from our factory or from another source. Once I had these parts in hand, I had to look them up in the *Fastener Standards* book and describe them by size. In other words, they wanted me to become familiar with all the products.

I was not in the warehouse long, and from there, I was sent to the back of the building where the factory was located. Again, I was not asked to learn to run any of the machines, only to understand what they did, see how they worked, and learn a little about raw material, tooling, and production times for the various machines. I learned how to read the production scheduling board, and eventually, I was exposed to the tooling and wire inventory. Reminder: Screws are made of wire.

My intent is not to make fastener experts out of my readers, but to give some information on how the industry works, and help you to picture the process. Plants buy huge coils of cold heading wire to make screws. The most common materials are carbon steel and stainless steel, brass, copper, silicone bronze, and aluminum, all of which come in various grades.

The appropriate diameter is ordered to run a particular part. The wire is automatically fed into a header machine, which as its name suggests puts the head on the screws. The part that comes out of the header is called a blank because it does not have any threads. The blank is rolled between two grooved blocks on a thread machine, or roller, that squeezes on the threads. Head slots for slotted screws and shank slots are cut into the threaded parts by machines called slotters. Now you are all fastener experts.

Now here is where the economics come in. The company I was working for was actually two companies in the same building. I guess this was for tax purposes. The factory was titled Jacob Screw, and the real company was titled Jacob Fastener Corporation. The only customer that Jacob Screw sold to was Jacob Corp.

The plant manager was a goofy guy. He was nice enough, I guess, but I felt that if people are that unhappy doing what they're doing, they should learn to do something else. But in his case, the options may have been somewhat limited.

I did learn the production scheduling board. I was exposed to manufacturing prints, to what operation each machine performed, and to some of the tooling needed to make parts; I also learned the production capacity of the various machines. I wasn't in the plant very long, but I was there long enough to inform our owner that he was getting screwed (ooh, there's another use of that word) by the raw material sources. One of the things I did in the factory was record the weight of the coils of wire and keep the inventory of raw material. It became obvious that they had been taking for granted the word of the suppliers that the weights on the coils or wire were accurate. They had never audited any of their shipments of wire. I didn't need to be an expert to weigh a coil of wire at 120 pounds and compare that to the 175 pounds on the tag.

"Huh," I said to myself, "that isn't the same." Being a good employee, albeit a newbie, I reported this discrepancy to the management. And being the new kid on the block, I was told by the factory manager that I was full of shit.

(At this point, I should point out to the reader that I have been accused of having issues with authority figures. This will become evident if you continue to read this book.)

I had already gone to the restroom that morning, and therefore I knew I was not full of shit, so I took it a step further and reported it directly to the owner. Did I mention that he was an emotional person? Oh, boy. He was not happy after he and I did some more inspecting. The company did not have a scale large enough to handle these huge coils of wire, so we had a platform scale installed to double-check the incoming wire shipments. Want to know how much credit I got for that? Nada.

As part of my training, I became a quality control (QC) inspector. This was my first but not my last QC job. I was able to save the company a lot of money by catching errors in the manufacturing process. After a few months, I had not made any money for the company. But I had saved them a ton. Was I praised to the sky? No, nothing, again.

Honestly, this was the best method for any company to train new employees. It is an investment, but it does reduce the number of mistakes they are going to make in the future. I assure you, sadly, this is not done today.

The next step in my education was to advance in the office and learn inventory control. In 1973, we didn't have computers; all of the product activity was posted by hand on a cardex system. Inventory control was then and is today considered the eye of the hurricane. The flow of every single part runs through this department. The posting of purchase orders, sales orders, and plant orders, and the flow of parts in and out of stock all were recorded by hand. If you are too young to know, a cardex system is a set of very thin drawers that have cards inside them that flip open so you can have information on the top card and the bottom card. It's extremely important to keep these records accurate. It takes a person who is perfect with this sort of record keeping. It truly was and is the heartbeat of the company. I also learned later that many companies utilized their cardex differently. I have seen numerous other methods over the years, but I really believe that we used the best, and the old company I mentioned earlier had broken into several offshoots. They all used the same system.

After a short stint in purchasing, I was moved to the inside sales desk. I was probably not ready for this. I had not been on any sales calls. I had no customer following at all. About this time, our purchasing agent left the company. Since I did have some experience, be it short, I was moved into the purchasing position. It was at this time that I came under the thumb of the equal partner in the company. Up until this point, my teacher, tutor, and guide was the principle owner. My new boss was a gentleman who had recovered from a massive heart attack. He had also been a graduate of that big company. He was not allowed to come to the office at all and was under a doctor's care for a long time. I had heard about him but had not met him until I had been employed there for a few months. He was to become my boss.

The responsibilities were divided among the principles. I have come to know that Fred was the best boss I would ever have. He was about five foot, eight inches tall and always claimed that he was a 210-pound tiger. When he was pretending to be angry, which he loved to do, he would ask if you had ever been attached by a 210-pound tiger. He was the fairest boss I ever had. He was very much a father figure to many of us. He was intelligent, demanding, aggressive, and very much a good guy. He had the ability to call you into his office and absolutely ream you a new one, but by the time you left his office, you felt like a million dollars. He was the first to joke around with you and really seemed to be one of the team rather than a dictator. Everyone who knew him loved him. His influence on anyone who worked for him was evident. He was the best.

My training went from the warehouse, to the factory, now to inventory control, a short stint in sales, and then to a permanent position in purchasing. I failed to mention the inventory control clerk. I used to say that if you looked up the term *fuddy-duddy* in the dictionary, his picture would be there.

Let me tell you a little about him. He passed away a few years ago, God rest his soul. He was a graduate of one of those old companies that went by the wayside many years ago. He was about five feet three inches tall, rather portly (but not fat), and a very snappy dresser. He always wore a white shirt and tie, a suit, or a sports jacket, and patent leather shoes. He talked with as slight lisp. He had snow white hair that he combed straight back. He was a very gentle man, who made very few mistakes. He did his job every day and was extremely loyal and dedicated. This made him an easy target for the low-life wise guys who worked around him. He was so easy to terrorize. It really was a lot of fun. I will give you a couple of examples of what we did to him.

His drink of choice was a sweet VO Manhattan. He also loved Delmonico steaks, which he grilled to medium rare. He had so many sayings that one of our salesmen began to keep a book titled *Famous Sayings,* or as we called it, the Book. He was such a fuddy-duddy that Larry, our PA, called him, "Rich the Bitch, tea-legged, bow-legged Rich."

Don, one of our inside salesmen and myself were of German ancestry. He frequently referred to us as "those dirty Germans." One time during lunch, he told Don that he had "a face for eatin' french fries" (Don was eating a burger and fries at the time). He always said that I was "born with a silver spoon in my mouth, with a loaf of bread under each arm, or knew where to get one." Make any sense? Not to me, but it must have to him. He made up songs and sang them to all the girls in the office, such as our receptionist, whose name was Donna.

He would sing, "Donna, dear, come over here and sit down by my window, window." No, you're right, it makes no sense, and he didn't have a window. But that was the beauty of Rich. Once, when there was a very slow period, when no one had gotten any raises, he suggested that we all could use one, and to get his point across to the office manager, he said, "Well, it looks like the Delmonico days are over."

The meanest things I personally ever did to him was to put a *Penthouse* magazine in the middle drawer of his cabinet. Now remember that he was quite a bit older than Don or me. He was very prim and proper. No one who knew him, would expect he would have a girlie magazine hidden in his desk. I already described the inventory cabinet. But there was also a pullout tabletop work area in front of each set of drawers and under a couple of these tabletop areas was a drawer for storage. This is where I put the dirty magazine. Oh course, he had no idea it was there. The trap was not quite set yet. If I was the one to discover it, the effect would have been worthless. If he was to find it, he could have just tossed it without saying anything. So to complete the proper results, I had my boss discover it.

Now, as I have already said, he was the best boss I ever had. He had a wonderful sense of humor, and I knew he would go along with a joke. I did not tell him what was in the drawer, only to "go see what Rich has in his drawer." He asked me what was going on. I told him to just go and look. I was not surprised that he went along with it, but I didn't know there was more to his willingness to go along than I knew.

My boss pushed and shoved his way around Rich and pulled open his drawer. This is something he would never ever do normally saying, "Rich, what the heck to you keep in here anyway?"

All the time, Rich was saying. Oh, geeeeeeeeee."

Then our boss pulled out the magazine and made a really big deal about it. He opened up the centerfold and showed it to everyone, including one of our secretaries, exclaiming how surprised he was that Rich would keep something like this in his drawer.

Then he said (much to my surprise), "What else do you have in there?"

At this point I was a little dumbfounded. To my knowledge, that was it. Our boss started rummaging through the drawer and came up with a package of prophylactics and said to everyone, "Oh, my God, Rich, what is this?"

The joke was getting better all the time. Rich kept claiming total ignorance. You see my boss, one of the owners of the company, had put them there himself, for the same reason I had put the magazine there. It turned out that he was as sick as the rest of us.

What kind of a boss was he? He was fair, educational, understanding, slow to anger, and always a good listener before making a judgment. I will tell you more about his managerial talents later.

One word of advice he gave me was, "Never, ever lie. Always tell the truth. It may hurt, but you will always remember the truth. People tend to forget lies."

Our sales manager/office manager was also one of the old guard. He was a real piece of work. He seemed to have some animosity against one of our inside desk salesmen. He did handle a major account, and that's probably why they kept him. He was rather heavyset and walked with a limp (he either broke or lost the big toe on one of his feet). The sick bastards in the office would imitate him by limping around the office, quacking like a duck. Yes, it sounds cruel, but there was no one more deserving. There was a strict rule that no one could eat at their desks. He always, not just sometimes, but always, had food stashed in the left-hand drawer of his desk; he'd lean over, take a bite, and sit up as if everything was normal. He often got caught, but it didn't make any difference to him; he would continue to do it anyway.

He was very protective of his coat hanger. Yes, I said his coat hanger. We had a coat closet that had wire hangers. He didn't like them, so he brought a wooden one from home for his coat. This was like showing blood to a bunch of sharks. Everyone used his hanger. It made him furious, so he would have to move the offender's coat to a wire hanger and put his on the wooden one. In an attempt to solve his frustration, he put a piece of white tape on the wooden hanger and wrote on it, "Property of Jim Smith. Keep your hands off." When it disappeared completely, he went nuts. I mean he was really mad that someone would steal his hanger. My old friend still has it, to this day. He evidently considers it something of a trophy or a fond memory of the good old days.

There are two other stories I want to tell you that illustrate how wonderful my boss was.

I graduated to purchasing when the current PA quit and went to another company. He couldn't stand working under our sales/office manager, who was a really good example of someone who is given power and instead of using it to enhance the company, he used it to belittle, embarrass, and browbeat the people under him. I was having my troubles with one of our main suppliers. This was the largest fastener company in the United States at that time. They set pricing standards that everyone used, and everyone bought from them. They had a catalog with published prices. They sold to other fastener companies on a list and discount basis, and your discount depended on how much business you gave them.

They had been a major supplier to us for many years. We had been selling bin seal bolts from them. These are fasteners used in making those large corrugated grain bins you see around the countryside. When I was doing the purchasing, that business had long since dried up. This major supplier had a huge warehouse locally, and almost all the companies in the United States relied on them for domestic parts. They were a quality company, and you could always rely on them, that is, unless you had to give them an order that had to be manufactured. I had inherited a group of orders that had been placed by the previous PA. They were all late; the expediting promises I had gotten had all turned out to be lies. Our obligation to our customers was getting later and later.

So I began to resource all of these parts so we could satisfy our orders. I began ordering these parts and then cancelling the overdue, late, and lied-to promises. I learned that we were not the only one of their customers that had this problem. Whenever you expedited one of your orders that was being manufactured, you were given a pat response of, "Another eight weeks." Whoever you talked to, you got the same answer. This was beginning to cause me some real problems.

I found other companies to get these parts from. Some were even at a cheaper price. I also discovered that the best way to get your parts from them was to make an order and then cancel it. I would get an expedited response that the delivery would take another six or eight weeks. I would place the order with another company, and the parts would show up a few days later. This really made me mad. If I didn't need the parts right away, I would reject them. After all, they had lied to me. This program seemed to be working out for me, until …

The general sales manager for this company showed up at our door. The saying was that if everything was going well, he would show up with a smile on his face. If things were not going so well, he was just nowhere to be found. I guess he didn't like controversy. So in the midst of my little program of cleaning up this mess, I get a call on my intercom from my boss, calling me into his office. Upon entering, there sat our smiling salesman, but there wasn't a hint of a smile. My boss asked me if I was cutting this longtime good supplier off.

I said, "Oh yes." He calmly asked me why. So I told him.

He asked to see some explanations for my actions. I went back to my office and grabbed the folder. When I returned, I spread out on my boss's desk each purchase order and the failed expediting promises, where I had placed replacement orders, many at lower prices. I did all this in front of the salesman. My boss politely asked me to leave and shut the door. I never knew what went on behind that door, but I had a pretty good idea. After the ace salesman left, I got called back into his office.

My boss said, "Steven, you didn't do anything wrong, except you didn't tell me what you were doing. I don't like surprises, so in the future, if you are going to cut off a supplier, would you please keep me informed?"

I told him I really didn't want to bother him with the details. He explained that he was proud of me for doing what had to be done, but he wanted me to keep him informed.

You might wonder why I would leave after only two and half years, especially since they had so many fun and interesting people. The answer is simple: I wasn't making any money. The owners were fairly young, early forties, and the manager was younger than them. The most important reason was we employees were often told that the management did not want to see the company get any bigger. That sort of limits a person's growth potential.

I mentioned that my predecessor had resigned due to friction with the office manager. I was beginning to have the same problems. Salespeople were constantly coming to see me. I had been attending association meetings and was also treated to numerous lunches. This put me in contact with a lot of folks in the business.

I will give the reader a little background on the local association. This was supposed to be a professional group of fastener companies. Back when it was first organized, the owners and top management would get together once a month. It developed into a bunch of the owners getting together to have dinner, play poker, and drink. There wasn't any real business conducted. Eventually, the purchasing agents for these companies decided to form their own group. This developed into a real organization, with real programs and real business relationships developed.

One of the products we did not make was sems, or an assembly of a screw and washer (sems, for short). At this time, there was only one company that was willing to sell them through distributors. The sales manager of their Distributor Sales department called on me numerous times. One day, while we were out having lunch, he said he wanted me to come to work for him as his assistant sales manager. This was a much larger company, with very aggressive people, and it had some real possibility for growth.

Therefore, like my processor, I gave my notice and moved on after two and a half years. I never forgot the education, experiences, and fun (sometimes) I had. The working conditions were getting intolerable for me, and I was now offered some real advancement, and so I took it. The only sad thing was that I was going to miss my boss. He had taught me so much about the business, so much about ethics, and one of the best things: how to handle paperwork. He said that if you handle a piece of paper correctly the first time, you won't see it again. If you don't, it will return and return and return. He also told me to never tell a lie. Lies are easily forgotten, and you will always remember the truth.

And to top off the class of the man, every time I ran into him after leaving the company, he would tell me he heard really good things about me and how proud he was of me. What a wonderful gentleman and a wonderful boss and a total class act. He passed away a few years later, after another heart attack. I will always have a soft spot for him.

CHAPTER 3

MOVING ON

It might be a good idea, at this point in my journey, to let you readers know that this is not a tell-all book. This is not intended to slander anyone. I will not go into any of the unfortunate things that can happen within a business. There won't be any mention of customers or parts sold or prices they were (or are being) sold for. My only purpose is to relate to you how strange this business is and some of the wonderful (and the not-so-wonderful) and yet weird people I have met and worked with over the past forty years and some of the really strange events I have been involved in. As I said earlier, the common joke around the industry is that once you get into it, it becomes a death sentence. You simply cannot get out of it. This, of course, is not true; there are thousands of people who have left this business, but to the ones who stay, this is what they tell the new people.

I will give you some examples of what I am saying. This is a very small industry; everybody knows everybody. If you are knowledgeable about the business and honest with people, there was security within the industry. I have gone out of my way (and sometimes made a pest of myself) to learn as much as I could about every facet of the business. This proved to serve me very well.

There are many professional fastener organizations around the United States. There is the National Fastener Distributors Association (NFDA). Then there are regional ones, the Southwest and Southeast (which likes to be known as the Fastener Association). There are ones in Los Angeles, Chicago, New England, and New York.

The one in New York is called the Metropolitan Fastener Association. For years, they held their meeting on the first Monday of each month, from September to June, at the Homestead in Manhattan. I used to go to the New York area quite often on sales trips, and I tried to time these trips so I could attend one of these meetings. The same people attended these meetings for twenty-five years. I will talk about the people in New York later. Early on, I hated trying to work with these people but learned to love them all dearly. They are the easiest to sell and some of the nicest folks to do business with.

There used to be only one large product show every year. It was more like a class reunion than a product show. You see, there is really very little that is new in the way of products from year to year, so there can only be a couple of reasons to go. One is to see old faces; another is to look for representation, or conversely, it is a great place for a rep to find a new principle. It is a good place to have a sales meeting with all your outside salesmen, again, because they are usually there to see industry customers or their principles.

Oh yeah, it's also a great opportunity to party. So why the hell did they have the first twenty of them in Columbus, Ohio? It is because the founder of the show lives there. I'm sorry; I don't mean to upset my friends in Ohio, but Columbus simply ain't Las Vegas, Chicago, Los Angeles, or New York, or Orlando, Florida. There isn't anything to do there. There aren't very many flights to Columbus from New York, Los Angeles, or Chicago, and since it's not a busy tourist area, the flights there are really expensive. The Ohio Center, where it was always held, is nice, I guess, but people who go to conventions or product shows also want to party. I do have some good stories about my twenty years of attending this show, and I will relate them in chronological order. They started in the late 1970s and have continued ever since, but wisely, it has now been moved to Las Vegas.

We need another aside here. In the fastener business, manufacturers are often asked by their customers to supply them with parts they cannot manufacture. So they act as any other distributor by supplying the OEM with distributed parts, right along with the product they manufacture.

Getting back to my story, I had been attending the association meetings as a purchasing agent. But since I was now an assistant distributor sales manager I was now attending these functions from a sales standpoint instead of purchasing. As I said earlier, back in the early 1970s, the association was a good ol' boys club. When I started attending the meetings, it was to the Purchaing agennts group. This became the real working association, and the party boys went by the wayside a few years later. This new working group had structured meetings and educational programs. We had elected officers and a board of directors. It was through these meeting that you would find sources for products you need to supply and establish personal relationships with men and women from other companies that can be of real service to you and, therefore, the company you worked for. Somehow, I became one of the members of the board of directors. I had not been elected to an office. Nor did I run for any of the offices.

With all the hopes of making this a real professional group, it certainly did have its growing pains. Some of the meetings did get out of hand.

On one occasion, we had a program with a handwriting expert. She was a very nice lady. Her presentation was professional and interesting. Unfortunately, two or three of our members had a little too much to drink. Shall I say, way too much. She was explaining how she became involved in reading handwriting, and one of these drunks yelled at her, "We don't care about that, get on with it."

Another time, at our annual dinner dance, we had hired a Jimmy Durante impersonator. This was a disaster. He was heckled horribly. It was terribly embarrassing, until he asked for a volunteer to join him on stage. He picked on one of the nicest guys, who had often been the brunt of many jokes around the office. He was short and rather meek. At first, he was really heckled, but to everyone's surprise, he was a total ham. He danced and joked, and the audience began to rave about him. He totally saved the evening. I have kidded him about that for years. I told him he missed his calling and should have been in show business

Another time, we were planning our annual dinner dance. The man who was the president at the time (he had actually campaigned for the position, and no one had ever done that) announced that the bar after the dinner would have to be a cash bar. This infuriated one of the members, who had already turned in a check for ten or twelve of his employees. He stood up and got into a heated argument with the president and ended up demanding his check back.

It got even more heated. Being on the board, I was seated at the dais next to the podium. I knew the situation was getting out of hand, so I literally took over the microphone and told the gentleman to settle down. I knew him very well, and I also knew he would be going, and he was only enjoying the show.

I said, "Settle down. If you are so upset over a drink, I'll buy you one."

His reply was, "Well, okay, if you're buying, here's my check back."

When I agreed to make this career change, the fastener industry had been in a terrible recession for several months, and we were just beginning to come out of it. I had some very limited exposure to OEM sales way back in my first job. I was in the Purchasing Department, where I learned the capabilities of many of the other fastener companies around the country. I was now hired to be the assistant distributor sales manager. The department was growing by leaps and bounds, and my boss wanted me to be able to manage the department, allowing him to travel around the country to work with our sales reps.

I worked there for the next eight and a half years. During this period in my career, I met some of the most bizarre characters I have ever known in my life. Most of them were employees, but others were reps we hired or were customers, and I met others who worked for different companies at trade associations.

Geographically, the first company I worked for was right near home, making it an easy commute. The second company was not. Way not. It was thirty miles away down on the South Side of Chicago. For you folks who do not know Chicago, for years, it was called the hog butcher of the world. The stockyard area was closed down, and only one slaughterhouse was in existence when I started working down there. The entire area had become an industrial park. It is now called the back of the yards.

Now there was also a cultural difference from where I lived. People who know the Chicago area know that there is a North Side, you know, Cub fans. Then there is the South Side, you know, Sox fans. The people who worked at here were either from the North Side, like me, or from the neighborhood. That would be the Canaryville/Bridgeport areas. To be perfectly blunt, this area was like a white island in a black sea, if you get my drift. The natives don't speak English. They use a lot of "dems," "dose," and "yous guys" (the translation for these terms are "them," "those," and "you guys." They are rough, sometimes pretty cold and unfriendly, very clannish. They have no idea that there is a world outside the neighborhood. I had to get used to an hour commute each way and learn how to get along with this new breed of human. To give you an actual example, a young man was shot helping a lady change a flat tire late one night. I asked about the police investigation. I was told they knew who did it, and they were going to take care of it. I think they meant it.

Iwill never forget my first day. I rode in with my new boss. The entire day was spent meeting everyone. My previous employer was a small company. The building was around twenty-five thousand square feet, with around twenty employees. This place had two thirty-five-thousand-square-foot buildings a block apart. One was the factory and office combination, and the other was just warehouse. The company employed fifty or sixty people. I would learn to love most of them, but if I thought that the characters at my first job were weird, I was in for a real rude awakening.

I need to start with my new boss. He was the distributor sales manager and first approached me and interviewed me; he was to be my boss for a few years. He spent much of that first day introducing me to all the people I would be dealing with. Some of them worked in the office, others in the warehouse, and still others in the factory.

I have learned over the years that every company, no matter what business they are in, has something about it that makes it unique. This place had so many, I will try to describe a few of them.

For instance, I learned early on that almost everyone changed their names. Why, I heard you ask? I never quite figured that out. The president, the VP, the plant manager, two of the salespeople, and the warehouse manager all changed their names. I had hired a really nice guy in sales, who happened to be from Thailand. His first name was difficult to pronounce, but not that hard. I was told to change it. We decided, as a joke, to change it to Lester. I asked him if he liked it.

He replied, "Have you ever known a Chinaman named Lester?"

Thankfully, we were allowed to let him keep his own name. But everyone in the company continued to call him Lester.

The president of the company was a bit of a character. I was told once that when advertising your product, you should never publish pictures of the management, that it's best to leave faces to the imagination of the person on the other end of the phone. He never got that message, or if he did, he ignored it. We published an annual catalog. Yep, you guessed it, a full page of him wearing the ugliest suit you could imagine, which became a standing joke around the industry.

One of our VPs was a really great guy. Guess who his first boss in the industry was? It was none other than my first boss. Right from the start, we had something in common. He felt exactly the same way about him as I did. Oh yeah, and going along with the common theme, he changed his name as well.

One of our managers was related to the original owner of the company. He was cut out of the will, so that might explain why he changed his name too. I won't mention either of them here.

There was an inside salesman in the OEM Department. Yes, he changed his name as well. His last name was difficult. Our PA, who, by the way, did not change his name, hired a very pretty girl in the Purchasing Department whose last name was Frost. Realizing that his last name was difficult he decided to change his last name to Frost. Right after I heard about this, I waited for him to come into the office, and when he did, I said, "How you doin', Jack?" He did not see any humor in it.

So not only was I introduced to all these new people and had to try to remember their names, but I was also given their real names along with the ones they wanted to use. It was all very confusing.

As the day progressed, I found it interesting of course, but everyone seemed nice and friendly, and I was beginning to think I had made a good decision. Around three o'clock, I was taken into the factory to meet Jim, the night superintendent, who managed the factory. It was explained to me that if I needed something done by the night shift, this was the guy who could make sure it happened.

A cold heading factory is very noisy, and it smells of burning cutting oils. Cold heading means there is no heat used to soften the raw material. But with the friction involved, the headed blanks that come off a cold header and the threaded parts that come off a thread roller are hot enough to be smoking. Hearing protection was not required back then, although it's a necessity today. OSHA requires it.

Most companies that have a second shift make that change at three o'clock. It was just before three, and there was Jim, the night superintendent, standing at the end of an aisle between two banks of thread rollers. Machines don't get turned off between shifts, so the noise was deafening.

As we approached him, he held up his hand and silently signaled for us to stop and mouthed, "Don't talk to me now. My day hasn't started yet." He pointed to his watch, pretended to count off the seconds, then raised both hands over his head, made wide circles, and yelled, "Okay, roll 'em!" He then calmly turned back to us and said, "Okay, now what can I do for you?"

We made our introductions, and he was informed that I was the assistant sales manager for the Distributor Sales Department. Jim turned to me, put his arm around me, and asked, "Tell me, Steven, how do you like it here so far?"

I told him how nice everyone seemed and how impressed I was with the factory and how pleased, overall, that I was to be working there. Little did I know that nearly every day for the next eight and a half years, he would greet me in exactly the same way. This became commonplace, so it wasn't long before I started interrupting him. The routine went something like this:

John would walk up to me and say, "Tell me, Steven ..."

Then I would interrupt him and say, "Tell me, Jim, how do you like it here so far?"

At this point he would hold his side, start to laugh and say, "Not too f— king good; sorry you asked."

There was another department head I need to describe to you.

Does anyone still smoke a pipe these days? I have known only one in twenty years. Let me tell you about him.

There were a few of us who worked down on the South Side and lived in the northern suburbs. We attempted to carpool from time to time. It would work for a while, and then for one reason or another, we'd get away from it. If you had the misfortune of carpooling with the pipe smoker, you had to put up with the smell. In his car, the ashes and disgusting pipe juice were all over the dashboard and floor. When he rode in your car, he would tamp out the ashes in your ashtray (seldom getting them actually in the tray), and then he would blow out the lovely juice on your carpeting.

He was one of the worst drivers in the entire Chicagoland area. He was either accelerating or braking. His right foot would be on the accelerator and his left on the brake. He never coasted. This means that you accelerated up to the car in front of you, until he slammed on the brakes to keep from hitting them. If you were in his car for any length of time, you became sick from the smell of old pipe smoke and tobacco drippings on the floor, or your nerves were a wreck from fear for your life. Your right leg is going to be in cramps from pressing the imaginary brake pedal on the passenger side of the car. Did I tell you he picks his nose? I'm sorry, I forgot that. What he was able to snag went under his seat (or yours, if it was your turn to drive). There is just one other thing that is rather scary about his driving; he tended to go into a trance and zone out from time to time.

If you are familiar with the freeway system in Chicago, you will know the area I am describing. Going out of Chicago on the Eisenhower Expressway, you come to an interchange where you can either go north on the 290 Eisenhower Extension, which merges with 355 North toward the northern suburbs, or go west, which becomes Tollway 88, which goes almost all the way to Iowa. Since all of us live in the northern suburbs, we always went north. He actually admitted to us that once while driving home by himself, he zoned out and ended up in Aurora before he realized that he missed his turn. Just think what it might be like to ride with him.

In the early 1970s, there was no penalty for sexual harassment. Around Halloween, the girls in the office always had a costume contest. It was always a lot of fun, and some of the costumes were really creative. I just happened to be in the warehouse a few days before the big event. The girls in the warehouse office were discussing their costumes, and I overheard part of their conversation. One of the girls was black; I didn't know her well, but she seemed a very nice lady.

The pipe smoker interjected and suggested to her, "I know, Mary; why don't you stick a broom handle up your butt and come as a fudge-sickle?"

I was totally appalled; you could have knocked me over with a feather. Everyone else who was there just stared at each other; they had an expression on their face that seemed to say, "Well, you have to consider the source."

His duties, at that time was warehouse manager. One day, when he was in the office/factory building, my assistant, a very good salesman and somewhat a character himself, walked up to him with a handful of rejected screws. He was a big guy, way bigger than our subject in question. He was asking whether to have the customer scrap the parts or return them for credit and replacement.

It happened to be a warehouse mistake and not a factory error. The office was very crowded at the time, and people were crowded around the cardex cabinets.

My assistant said, "What should I do about these?"

Our buddy took one look and hit his hand, scattering the screws all over the office. Now, my assistant was a wonderful guy with a great sense of humor, but he was about six feet three and weighed close to two hundred and fifty pounds. The entire office went silent, and everyone looked at them, wondering what was going to happen. Many of them were hoping he would just deck him. Others were hoping he wouldn't, fearing it would result in him losing his job. The silence was deafening, and the suspense was killing us. He first looked shocked and then a little embarrassed, and obviously a little angry.

He settled himself, leaned calmly against the inventory cabinet, and said "Now, wasn't that childish?" His response couldn't have been more perfect.

This was about the time that everyone was becoming computerized. The company consolidated under one roof and expanded to become one large firm, one that was well known in the industry. We had joined fastener associations all around the country. Most of them had at least one major function. We attended as many of them as we could, giving us the most exposure.

The idea of putting our favorite warehouse buddy in charge of the new computer project did not seem like a good idea. Surprisingly, it was a stroke of genius. He did a wonderful job at it, but he often stepped out of bounds with people, verbally. He made me so angry some days that I went to my boss to see if I had to answer to him or not. I was told that I did NOT work for him. So on my way back to my office, I popped my head in his office, got his attention, and told him to go f—k himself. He looked confused, but I really felt better.

Why am I so hard on him? Easy: He deserved it. He could also be one of the nicest people you could ever know. If you needed help or were in real trouble, if he could help, he would go out of his way to help. At times, it seemed like he had a heart of gold. Unfortunately, if he did help you, you would hear about it the rest of your life. By the way, if you offered to buy him a cup of coffee, he would always say, "No, but I'll take the twenty-five cents." That was not a joke. He meant it.

As I said, he was given the job of establishing the computer system IBM was developing for us. No one had any knowledge of computers. No one.

This is what he did: He went to all the department heads, gave each one of us a spiral notebook, and told us to meet with our departments and do a lot of soul-searching. In a week, we were to have listed everything we wanted the computer to do. Most of us had no idea what computers were capable of, and we told him so. He told us to assume that computers can do anything and to list our desires, and not to be conservative in any way. He then took all these reports from the various departments and put them altogether.

When he met with the IBM representatives, he told them to set up a software system that could do it all. He also told them, in his usual fashion, that it had to be "simple enough that a monkey could work it or better yet, any idiot off the street." Because that is what he thought that is what we had working there, a bunch of idiots. What they came up with was the most user-friendly software system the fastener industry ever saw.

It allowed the salespeople in both the Distributor Sales Department and the OEM departments to handle three to four times more calls, more efficiently, and more accurately than ever before. I have been exposed to a few other fastener software systems since then, but none came close to this; it put all the information you could ever want at your fingertips, and instantly.

CHAPTER 4

MANAGEMENT

A little aside here: When a person decides to change jobs in this goofy industry, it is always assumed they were stolen, as if someone put a gun to their head. My boss and I were almost the same age. This was the only fastener company he had ever worked for. He loves to talk. I do as well, but from a sales standpoint, this can be a good thing, or it can be a bad thing. If a potential customer won't talk to you, it can be difficult to judge how much to push. I'll give you an example: I was on an OEM sales call with one of our outside salesmen. This was very unusual, since I was in distributor sales. During one call, he did all the talking; I thought it had been a good call, but it seemed to me that he cut it short. I asked him why, and he said he was watching the body language of the buyer. He started looking at things on his desk and seemed to be losing interest. He told me that was a signal to pack up and leave.

Even a better example was a call my assistant and I made on one of the largest fastener distributors in the country. I had decided that my new assistant would personally handle this account. I wanted him to meet the people in the quotation department as well as the people who would be doing the purchasing. That was all completed, and we were about to leave. I thought it would be good for him to meet the owner and asked the receptionist if he could see us. She said that he could.

After we entered his office, I introduced him to my assistant and asked him to explain how his company functioned. We had trouble making rush deliveries from stock. It sometimes took a few days. The company he was going to be servicing always shipped parts the same day the order was taken. I wanted my assistant to hear this from the man himself.

That was the last thing we said until forty-five minutes later, when we thanked him and left. As we were walking out the door, the buyer flagged us down and demanded to know what we had done. She said that no one, absolutely no one, was ever in the owner's office that long; the entire company was in an uproar. She wanted to know what in the world was going on.

I told her, "Nothing. I just asked him to explain how his company worked."

The lesson here is, if the customer wants to do the talking, let him. After you leave, he will think you're the best salesman he's ever met.

One of the fellows in the carpool gang, we'll call him Greg, had known our warehouse guy longer than the rest of us northsiders. I began to believe he had learned to drive from him, as well. Greg didn't smoke a pipe, thank God, and he didn't try to run up on the bumper of the car in front of him, but nevertheless, it was a real adventure to ride with him. There are many examples of how he drove; here are just a few.

One morning in the carpool, I was sitting in the back seat, our purchasing manager was driving, and Greg was riding shotgun. Traffic on the inbound Kennedy Expressway was terrible. He was trying to change from the middle lane to the right lane so he could make the upcoming exit. No one would let him in. He had his turn signal on, he had slowed down, he was looking and hoping for someone to be kind enough to let him in, but to no avail.

Greg said to him, "Are you trying to get over?" He said he was, so Greg told him to get ready. Our driver said, "Get ready for what?"

Suddenly, Greg opened the passenger door, all the way. Yes, we were traveling about sixty-five miles per hour. He then yelled, "Okay, now, go!"

He had thrown his door open between two cars on the expressway. Of course, the one behind the open door slammed on his brakes, allowing us to change lanes. I was sitting in the back seat in total terror.

On another occasion, Greg was driving, I was in the passenger seat, and my friend was in the back. Now, for you readers who are not familiar with the expressway system in Chicago, if you are inbound on the Kennedy, you can't enter the express lanes. This is because they start on the inside lanes, just after the merger with the Edens Expressway. Edens drivers are allowed to use the express lanes, but the Kennedy cars would have to cross four lanes to use them, and that's not allowed. The only barrier keeping you from doing this are the multitude of warning signs and a double yellow line. It is patrolled very closely, and cars are ticketed all the time for trying to make this little maneuver. No problem for Greg. He just jumped over the double yellow lines, and all four lanes of traffic, and into the express lanes, as if it was the most natural thing in the world to do. Both of his passengers told him that the penalty for doing that was something between five to ten years. He played completely innocent, as if he didn't know he couldn't do it.

Now, again, to further explain, there are no entrances or exits from the expressway until the lanes merge back into the Kennedy, just before you enter the Loop (that's the downtown area, for you non-Chicagoans). Well, the traffic backed up and slowed to a crawl. Greg started looking over his right shoulder and then back in front of him. I wondered what he was looking at; what was he trying to do? Then I noticed that up ahead about a quarter of a mile, the guard rail went away, and the only barrier between the express and local lanes was a one-foot-high curb.

I thought and then said out loud, "No! No, you're not going to do this."

Ignoring me, he jumped the curb and went back into the local lane. The poor guy he edged in front of was so shocked, his hair was standing straight up. Both passengers were yelling at him that he was f——ing crazy. He, again, was as calm as can be and said that if he were to be stopped by the police, he would merely say he felt so guilty about getting into the express lanes illegally back at the start that he thought he would get back in the locals down here.

Sometimes, we took the Eisenhower Expressway instead of the Kennedy. We usually got off at Independence Boulevard and proceeded into work, using what is referred to as the boulevards. This includes Independence, Douglas, Sacramento, Marshall, California, and Western. Greg considered this route his own personal Indianapolis Speedway. He would take these sharp curves at speeds up to seventy miles per hour. But the topper to all these stories was one I wasn't involved in, thankfully. Greg, the PA, and another salesman all had a little contest to see who could get to Melrose Park the quickest. They all took their own favorite routes; as they got closer to their destination, the PA was in the lead, but they all ran into some road construction; all lanes were blocked and a flagman was directing only a few cars at a time to pass from each direction. There was no way around it. They were really close to their goal. All was lost for Greg, or so it seemed. He noticed there wasn't any construction on the sidewalk so, you got it, he jumped the curb, drove down the sidewalk, went around the construction, and won the race.

I'm supposed to be telling you about management, so here is some more. The president of the company, one of the people who changed his name, was a snappy dresser and liked to claim that he was the original owner. The company actually started two years before he joined as a minority partner. But being the egomaniac he was, he would claim there wasn't any company before he got there. Ego is a strange thing; all of us have some, and it's not a bad thing. But I have always been taught that anything in excess is a bad thing, and, well, enough said.

The first day I worked there, he thought it would be fun to tape down the button on my phone, which was rather cute, I guess.

We had monthly manager's meeting at a local rat- and cockroach-infested restaurant/bar. These were supposed to start at noon. He would show up around one, hoping we all had enough drinks to speak our minds. He was always a micro-manager. Whatever crossed his desk often became a logjam. One day, before he showed up, we decided to suggest that he stay in his office and let his management team do their jobs unabated. Evidently, this was not what he was expecting. He blew up. He went into a tirade and ended by saying he would agree to this for six months, and if the results were not to his liking, we were all fired. Over the next twelve months, our sales doubled.

The plant manager (yes, he had changed his name as well) was one of the original owners and had long ago sold his shares. Stanley was a big, burly man who had always been a factory guy. He knew manufacturing and could be difficult to work with, for a lot of people. I, on the other hand, loved talking to him and have many fond memories of him.

The first one was when I had taken an order for a nonstandard part from our largest distributor customer. I had not asked anyone from the factory if we could run it. Stanley was furious. My good friend, the PA, was upset because he had to try to get another company to run them for us cheap enough that we would not lose too much money. My boss was understanding but insisted that I get a better handle on what our factory could and could not manufacture.

I felt really bad, especially for making Stanley angry. I went to his office to apologize, and we talked about the part. I told him there was no way in the world I would ever go around him, and the only reason I had taken the order was that at my previous company, we ran similar parts all the time. I assumed we could run something similar.

This surprised him, I guess. He asked me if they really made parts like this. I said certainly; otherwise, I would have asked him before I quoting it. He called one of our best header men into his office. A few hours later, I was working at my desk, not looking up, when a still-very-warm blank (a headed screw with no threads on it) was tossed onto the middle of my desk. I picked it up and started to examine it. Realizing that it was my infamous part, I looked up slowly, and there was Stanley, with this big grin on his face.

I said, "Damn, it is a shame we can't run these."

33

Stanley said, very gruffly, "Come with me."

I followed him into his office.

He sat me down and said, "Steven, I want to thank you for shaming me into trying something I didn't think we could do."

He showed me that he was a gentleman as well as a stern boss. This was the start of a very nice relationship for many years to come.

For many years, he had to put up with tools disappearing from our factory. Somehow, mystically, they just seemed to walk out the door. One day, he decided to solve this problem. He loved the color yellow and had all the tools in the factory painted yellow. It was a standing joke that there were yellow tools all over the South Side of Chicago.

In the late 1970s and early 1980s, there was a run on silver. People were cashing in their old silver coins and getting a return of 10 to 1. My friend had a friend who bragged that he never spent a dime. He had a narrow-necked jar next to his fireplace and had been throwing real silver dimes in it for years. He cashed them in for a very tidy sum.

Stanley was a collector of all sorts of things, including coins. I had a few that were worth more than their face value and was talking to him one day about coins and the exchange rate. He told me he probably would cash in his silver coins that were duplicates, thinking that they probably would never be worth more than they were then. I agreed with him and casually asked him if he had his collection in a safe deposit box in a bank. He laughed and said the bank he used didn't have one large enough. I told him the one I rented was small but my bank had some really large drawers.

He again said, "No, they don't have anything large enough."

I asked him, "How much do you have in silver coins?"

His reply shocked me. I strongly suggested that he not tell anyone else, but he didn't seem concerned at all.

This brings me to my good friend, the PA. Since he looked like Clint Eastwood, I'll just call him Clint. Yes, he did look a lot like the famous movie star. From the very start, he and I carpooled for a long time. He would drive one day and I the next. He was divorced at the time and lived in an old speakeasy from years past. He had a roommate he rarely saw. But more importantly, he had just purchased a little Irish setter puppy. I had just bought a collie puppy. They were nearly the same age. Every day I drove, he would be running late. To hurry us along, I would feed Charlie. You know, the way to a dog's heart is through his stomach. I became Uncle Stevie. Clint decided to campaign Charlie. That means entering him in dog shows, and he became one of the highest rated setters in the country. He never forgot Uncle Stevie. He loved to put his paws on each of my shoulders and then chew on one of my ears. God, I do love dogs.

I said he resembled the famous actor. Let me mention an example. We usually stopped for coffee at a local 7-Eleven. One morning, the check-out girl actually asked him if he was Clint Eastwood. I really wish he had said yes, but he told her no. I was laughing so hard, he had to drag me out to the car.

I guess if you are good looking and single, you get introduced in various ways to some rather lovely young ladies. (Holy crap, that is an understatement.) Honestly, he went out with some of the prettiest girls I've ever seen. Keep in mind that most of them were considerably younger than him. If fact, this became grounds for a lot of good-natured kidding. We were going to lunch one day and noticed some junior high girls walking near their Catholic school, wearing matching uniforms. It wasn't me, but one of the guys in the car pointed one out to Clint, like, maybe he could get a date with her.

He was probably the fairest manager at the company. He had the largest department, and everyone who worked for him swore he was the best. I don't doubt it at all. He and I have been friends for nearly forty-five years now. So here is this kind, loving, gentle, fair, good-looking guy; whoa, slow down.

Let me tell you about the car I bought as a second car for my ridiculous commute. I was traveling nearly thirty miles, one way, and needed my own car. The department heads all had company cars. They got new ones every three years. I really needed a second car, so I made a deal with our controller to painlessly inherit one of the three-year-old company cars. It was a 1972 or 1973 Chevy Impala. It had a lot of miles, but they were all expressway driving.

However, there were a few little things about it. Like, there was this crease between the two left headlights that continued straight down through the bumper. This was a result of a combination of a very late night and a stop sign. There was a dent in the door that was the result of a temper tantrum. The ashtray was broken and wouldn't close properly, again the result of another temper tantrum. The emergency brake lever was pulled all the way out and then twisted and bent underneath the dashboard. It really is maddening when it catches the cuff of your pants and tears them. Just think how much strength that would take. I think I did say that I didn't pay much for it, right?

CHAPTER 5

THE REST

Middle management is hard: trying to get orders in a very competitive industry, manage a department, approve all orders, work on setting up a branch warehouse, establish all published prices, and keep everyone happy both above me and below, as well as hiring, firing, and managing our distributor sales reps.

The Purchasing Department had a number of women. They were taught to handle our direct importing, which was a job in itself. Two other men worked in the Purchasing Department; one I'll call Fred had worked in the industry for many years. The rumor was that he liked his liquor. In fact, the rumor was that we never saw him sober. I can't confirm that. He was always very nice to me, and the manager thought the world of him. He did everything in slow motion, but I'm also told that he never made any mistakes. He did seem to know everybody in the industry.

Another story about my assistant involves a man from the Purchasing Department; we'll call him Ben. He worked there for nearly as long I had, but I didn't have much contact with him. I assumed he was a good employee, or he would have been let go. As I said earlier, I don't think I ever had an issue of any kind with him. I am told that other people did, but I had no knowledge of it while I was working there. The probable reason is that the Distributor Sales Department never jobbed anything (that is, buy for the purpose to sell something) the OEM Department did all the time. The only parts we sold were made in our factory. There is an old saying

(I think I made it up): "You can't job to a jobber." We only sold parts that we made. So Ben dealt only with the OEM Sales Department. Clint was always very supportive of his department. That is a very good thing.

It always seemed to me that, the man we'll call Ben always seemed rather strange. But I never thought that he was dangerous. But one day many years later, I was working for another company. A very good friend and supplier came to call on me. He told me that he was making a sales call at my old company. They had met in a conference room, and Ben went crazy, totally nuts. He threw chairs around the room, screaming and yelling, and claimed that he was going to get a gun and kill the two co-presidents of the company, one of which was my dear friend Clint. I was shocked, of course, and called my friend at once and warned him that he had a nut case on his hands. He assured me not to worry, it was just Ben letting off steam. I tried to tell him that this was not something to just shrug off. He insisted that I had nothing to worry about.

A few days later I was on the phone with my old assistant, who was now the sales manager, and told him about the incident. He proceeded to tell me that it was probably true. Then he told me about another one of his antics.

Ben had begun a habit of getting up from his desk at exactly 3:27 every afternoon, leaving his coffee cup on a file cabinet, going into the men's toilet, and standing at the urinal with his pants dropped all the way to the floor; after finishing, he'd wash his hands, going back into the office, pick up his coffee cup, and return to his desk. This had become such a ritual that everyone in the office would check their watches by him.

One day, he got up from his desk at the usual time, dropped off his cup, and went into the men's restroom. My old assistant quickly got up and put the cup inside the file cabinet; he shut the drawer and went back to his desk. When Ben returned from doing his duty, he reached for his cup, as he always did, and found it missing. I guess he went nuts. I am told he went ballistic, yelling, screaming, swearing, accusing anyone and everyone of stealing his cup. Nobody paid him any attention or even looked up from their work. Nobody acknowledged him at all. He ran out into the factory, screaming that he was going to kill whoever took his cup. While he was in the factory, you-know-who returned the cup to the top of the file cabinet, exactly where Ben had left it. Then he quickly returned to his desk and sat down.

In came Ben, still in a rage, still screaming, and in midscream, he noticed his cup right where he had left it. Seeming very confused, he reached for his cup and stared at it in his hand. Now, was this the end of he story? Of course not! At this very moment, our culprit stood up and said, "Hey Ben, you got a problem with that cup?"

Again, no one looked up or took any notice. The only sad thing about this story is that I wasn't there to witness it personally.

Our controller was always considered the eye of the hurricane. In fact, he said so himself. By that, I mean he didn't let anything upset him. The president would be going nuts, causing others around him to be upset, but he was always cool and calm. He loved going to Las Vegas two or three times a year (and probably still does). He loved to gamble and told me he only played craps. He was good at it, and he would win. He had a system that worked for him. He readily admitted that you needed luck with his system. He explained that the odds are always against you with every game out there, but with craps, the odds are constant. There are only six sides on a die, and there are only so many combinations that can come up. Evidently, he was lucky because he did win a lot. He told me he was extremely regimented in his system. He was very strict in the rules that he set for himself.

So here is this disciplined CPA, a very steady rock of a person. He referred to himself as the eye of the hurricane. He had a system for playing craps that he stuck to. Get the picture?

He called me into his office after he returned from one of his trips to Vegas and said, "Steven, I was standing at the craps table, and things were just so-so. I was pretty much even on the night. I looked across the table, and they gave the dice to a very pretty girl, and I saw this aura all around her.

I know that she was blessed. I loaded the table, and she proceeded to make twelve passes. I stayed with her for nine of them."

The girl was betting five dollars at a time, and after she finally crapped out, he handed her a thousand-dollar chip and said, "Thank you, honey."

While he was telling me this story, his eyes got wide and he was kind of in a daze. I told him he was full of crap. He swore it was all true, but he also won twenty-four thousand dollars that night, so I guess he may actually have a gift, after all.

I mentioned this to our plant manager, who also loved to play craps. Unfortunately, he always lost. He went to our controller repeatedly and pleaded with him to teach him his system. Our controller always refused because he knew he was too emotional and not disciplined enough to follow it. He continued to plead his case, so he finally agreed to go over it with him. Our controller sat him down in his office, had him take out a piece of paper, and wrote down the system. About halfway through the process, he began to argue that it wouldn't work.

The controller got so angry that he threw him out of his office, screaming at him, "Go to Vegas, lose your money, be happy."

We needed a new warehouse manager, and the search was on. When one of the applicants, we'll call him James, entered the warehouse, he said he didn't think he was the man for the job. I need to mention here that James is black. When asked why, James said if he was hired, there was going to be a problem, because he was not going to work in a "pigsty." He said before he would ship anything out of the warehouse, there was going to have to be some serious housecleaning.

Guess who we hired? You are correct. The first month James was with us, he turned the warehouse into a place we could be proud to take any customer through, along with having a record shipping month at the same time. The warehouse, out of protest, had become unionized, but that didn't bother James. He proceeded to handpick his own crew from the neighborhood and ended up with a really good team. He was never able to get rid of the union, but he was respected by everybody, and our Shipping Department was very well run.

One of his handpicked employees was a real character. I never knew his real name; we called him Uh-Font (that may have been his real name, for all I know). The only real job I ever saw him do was janitorial. He swept the floor of the warehouse and did various odd jobs. I never saw him pull parts or pack parts for shipment. He wore a different cap every day. He also made himself the unofficial greeter. He had a gift of gab that was second to none. He told me that prior to coming to work for us, one of his jobs was to sweep out Comiskey Park after all the White Sox games. He claimed to be the best sweeper in the city of Chicago. If you were walking through the warehouse, you would inevitably get cornered by Uh-Font for the latest news. He would also greet anyone you escorted around the warehouse and discuss the world news with them.

The union had gotten a foothold in the warehouse due to personnel issues in the past. With James's new group, there was really no need for a union. There was an effort to remove the union, but it failed by one vote. That vote came from Uh-font. He hated the union as well as the union steward. So why would he vote to retain it? Because that same union steward cornered him with a forklift in the back of the warehouse, away from anyone else's view, and threatened that if the union was not retained, he was going to be blamed for it and was going to be made to pay.

The company continued to grow, and we moved into a hundred-sixty-five-thousand-square-foot building a few blocks away. Having everything under one roof made life much simpler. But since the warehouse was unionized and the factory was not, this posed a problem. The answer was to build a wall. Yes, a cement block wall between the two, and no one on the warehouse side was allowed to cross over to the factory side. I really doubted that it would work. But it must have, because the factory never did become unionized.

I already described the night factory foreman. Let me describe our daytime manager. He was a very good roller man in his own right. He was protective of his factory workers. He was a cranky old Irishman who had lived on the South Side his entire life. For you folks who are not familiar with Chicago, the city is full of small areas that are very clannish; some areas hate other areas, and they have vocal accents that distinguish one area from another. He was typical of the people who live on the South Side. They know where everything is south of the Eisenhower Expressway, but are completely lost north of it. I'll give you an example.

Every summer, the association had a golf outing. It was held at various golf courses in the area, but it has always been on the northwest side. For years, it was held at the Itasca Country Club, which is in Itasca, a suburb just west of O'Hare Airport. It's not easy to find. Now mind you, he had played in this outing for years. But someone else always drove him there. He was given detailed instructions, but going north on the Tri-State 294, he missed his exit and just kept going north. Somewhere close to the Wisconsin border (or maybe after he saw the sign announcing, "You are now entering Wisconsin"), he realized he went too far.

Instead of stopping and calling someone, he turned around and started heading back. He went all the way to the South Side, where he felt comfortable, and then called for help. He then turned back north and followed the instructions, finally getting to the outing just in time for dinner. He had to have traveled a hundred and fifty miles out of his way. The southsiders always tease us north siders that we don't know how to get around down there. But drop them off anywhere north of the Ike, and they're really lost. By the way, if you have ever driven in the Chicago area, you know it is one of the easiest cities to find your way around.

CHAPTER 6

SALES

Keith was an older gentleman in the OEM Sales Department.

Did I explain what OEM stands for? I'm sorry, it stands for Original Equipment Manufacturer. In other words, the end user of the parts.

He was very much like the older gentleman who worked the inventory at my first employer. In fact, they worked together way back in the fifties. Keith lived with his mother and had never been married, although he did have a longtime girlfriend. He was a very snappy dresser and was a very strange little guy. One time, he called into work early one morning and asked to speak to his boss, the OEM sales manager. He told him he couldn't make it into work in his own car and could someone come and pick him up. He was, of course, asked what the problem was. You see, he had backed his car out of his garage and shut the garage door on the hood of his car. He did not have an electric garage door opener; he did it by hand. He was so flustered, he didn't know what to do.

Another time, he borrowed his boss's briefcase to go on a sales trip. The next morning, he was leaving for work and had another little garage problem. He put the briefcase down and then backed his car out over it. The briefcase got caught in one of the wheels and got jammed up inside the wheel well, preventing the car from going anywhere. Again, he needed a ride to work.

Keith loved to tell jokes. The problem was that he often flubbed up the punch line. It got so silly; everyone knew he did this, and the goofed-up punch line would be funnier than the joke he was trying to tell. Here is an example:

"Did you hear about the guy who went to the drive-in theater and froze to death?" Here's the punch line. The title of the movie was *Closed for the Summer.* (No, the title was *Closed for the Winter.*)

Sales meetings were always an interesting time. The reader has already figured out there were two sales departments, one to sell parts to other fastener companies, and one to sell to OEMs. This often caused some stress. At one of these meetings, the OEM sales manager complained that our enormous inventory was loaded with only distributor parts. My boss yelled back at him, "And they [the distributors] sell them to your customers."

We often ran into distributor customers who were afraid we were cutting them out of their customers by selling direct. This was absolutely impossible. My department was so busy, there was no way we would have the time to cross-check anything. In fact, we discovered there were hundreds of instances where distributors were buying parts from us and selling them to our OEM customers.

Then there was the assistant OEM sales manager. He was a very good salesman and knew the industry well. He had worked for other companies and was very knowledgeable but loved to stir up trouble. He would go out of his way to learn what pissed people off and goad them into getting upset. If he could make enough trouble that a fight would ensue, he was in his glory. Frankly, I learned to really hate office politics and always tried to keep away from them. Selling is a very pressure-filled job, and in every case, for every company, in every business, sales is pressure packed. If you don't sell, you are going to be looking for a job somewhere else. I have always been concerned with getting the order, making sure it is profitable, and seeing that it gets shipped on time. If we, as salespeople, get that done, we are usually in a good position to get the order the next time it comes due. If something goes wrong, and one of those things doesn't happen, you may not get a repeat order (and maybe not any more orders for anything).

It sounds pretty simple, but it isn't. Muddying the water with the bullshit that so many people get involved is nonproductive and can become cancerous. This stuff has always upset me. I always love a good joke and love to play little tricks on people and have them pulled on me. It lightens the atmosphere and keeps the pressure from getting too bad. But to go out of your way to cause friction is divisive, counterproductive, and a waste of time.

I need to get serious here for a moment. Middle management is not easy. You have the folks you are supposed to manage and keep happy. Then you have the folks you must answer to, and you better make sure they stay pleased with your department's performance. I was raised by an army major. He was very direct. He didn't mince words. He would give you an order, and it had better be obeyed. So as an adult, I didn't have any problem with being given a duty. When I first started here as assistant sales manager, I wrote up an order and thought it was a good order, but my boss had a question about it. This is how he handled the situation: He asked me to sit down, handed me my order, and said, "Tell me about this." Instead of merely asking why I did such-and-such, he put me on the defensive.

I don't think he expected my response. I answered him by saying, "What's wrong with it?"

I always felt that being direct is the best way to handle a situation. Don't waste words or time. If a mistake has been made, fix it. Get on with business. No real harm has been done. Get on with getting orders. No feelings hurt. No one has been offended or felt uncomfortable.

This got me into trouble. After my boss left the company, I was promoted to the manager. One of the men in my department screwed up an order. It was really not a big deal. I knew the order would not pass final inspection. I just handed it back to him and literally whispered to him to fix it. This was a very meek and mild guy, and he was crushed.

To give the reader another example, I had to do the same thing to my worthy assistant. As I walked by his desk, I laid the order on his desk and said something like, "This won't fly." He took a look at it and said something like, "Oh crap." I learned that you have to treat everyone differently.

The department wrote eight thousand orders a year. This was a department of six. This gives you some idea of how many phone calls we took and how many quotes we had to make on a daily basis. We did not have time to waste discussing questionable orders. I had to approve the orders before they were processed. I was not the last person to approve them.

We had a couple of interesting sales reps. For those of you who don't know what that is, I'll explain. These are independent agencies that sell your product, as well as other nonconflicting products. You pay them a percentage of the sale price. There are good reps who are worth their weight in gold to you. Sadly, these are few and far between. Then there are the ones that collect lines, often so many that they can't do justice to any of them. I have experienced both.

I had one who had been asked by our management to attempt to get us into some OEM customers. He was well known by the distributors in his territory and felt if they found out he was calling on any OEMs, they would blackball him. He resigned. He was a good rep, and I told him he was foolish for doing so. I had to replace him and found out that the best way to hire a good rep was by asking your best customers to suggest one. That is how I got one of the best guys I ever worked with. I have a wonderful story about him that occurred much later, after I moved on to another company.

All good things come to an end, and my tenure there ended after nearly nine years. The circumstances were unfortunate and unnecessary, but they all worked out for the best. I promised not to go into bad things, so I won't.

CHAPTER 7

FINALLY, NEARER HOME

I related a story about the fellow who got into a brouhaha over the tickets to a dinner dance. Well, he and I became pretty good personal friends. On my way out of the city for the last time, I stopped off at the company he ran. I told him what had happened, said what a surprise it had been, and asked what I should do now? I had yet to ever look for a job.

Another aside just for information:

You readers should know that the fastener business is broken down into many smaller subdivisions. There are fewer and fewer companies that actually manufacture parts, due to foreign competition. Prior to the 1970s, there were a lot of manufacturers. Cold heading machines are very expensive, and it requires a skilled set of workers to run them. One of the problems in our industry is the lack of training of young workers to replace the skilled ones who retire. But companies that manufactured fasteners can't make everything. Decisions were made by each company, as they grew, as to what machines they would buy, based on what their customers demanded. Therefore, in many instances, the direction a manufacturer went depended on what their customer base required.

This was not the case with socket products. Socket parts require very specialized machines as well as materials, tooling, and specifications. So today, we have companies that only make socket products such as socket cap screws, set screws, plugs, hex keys, and other socket-related parts. We have washer companies that require stamping machines that have nothing to do with cold heading. And within that branch of the business, you have companies that make only flat and conical spring washers and others that only make tooth washers, like internal and external tooth washers. There are other washer companies that only make split ring washers. You have companies that make wire-related products like cotter pins. Beyond these, you have screw machine companies that make very special parts, one at a time, that are milled from bar stock. So manufacturing is usually specialized to a degree.

Now, you might ask why an OEM wouldn't buy these parts from the people who make them? Simple, as you should know by now, fasteners are cheap. Especially compared to what your company makes. You can call one supplier and give them all your fastener requirements. Combine the shipments, combine the invoices, and just make sure everything is there on time so you keep your factory running. Are you beginning to get how important the Purchasing Department is? As my first boss said, "Real profit is made in the Purchasing Department."

I could write an entire book on my friend who ran this socket company. In fact, I might just do that. If I gave you his real name, he might sue me; he might even kill me. He might just get a good laugh out of it, but I will leave him nameless for now. My first exposure to him was toward the end of my first job. I was doing the purchasing at that time and began attending the association meetings. Back then, the meetings were always held at a large restaurant that was centrally located.

I told you a little about him earlier. He was the guy that argued about the cash bar verses an open bar at one of our diner dances. He had become a good personal friend, and ignoring his antics in public, when he had an audience and could perform, he was a super guy.

I had not had to apply for any job at this point, at least not in the fastener business. I came to expect potential employers to ask, "What can you bring with you?" Meaning, do you have customers who love you and you can bring along to us? Thanks to my father's upbringing and my first boss's rule, never to tell a lie, I always replied, "Not a dime. I can promise you my ability, my hard work, and my talents." No one can promise business. In fact, whenever that question was asked of me, I immediately felt that I didn't want to work under that kind of pressure.

But now, I was in a position where I had to look for a job. I had gotten caught in a political mess I never wanted or asked for. All I wanted to do was sell screws, preferably to distributors I had grown to know and love. I loved the people I had worked with for nearly nine years, and I loved the customers, the reps I had worked with around the country, and the branch office. With the many professional organizations, we belonged to around the country, and the friends I had made in those travels, I felt I had learned a lot about sales, management, manufacturing, and the technical aspects of the business. I had not forgotten that old fastener saying that there is no such thing as job security in this business, but there is security within the industry, if you have something to offer.

Alright, I am going to give you readers a little knowledge of this screwy business. I have to ask you to bear with me.

At one time, all screws were milled from bar. This is done by cutting bar stock into little individual screws. In this method, you have from 50 to 70 percent scrap. The molecules within the material that are lined up to start are still lined up with cut off lines, leaving them very weak. Production in this method is very slow, maybe one to five parts per minute, depending on how intricate the part is. In cold heading, you feed a coil of wire cold (thus cold heading) into a machine that cuts off the correct length of wire, transfers it to a die, and forces it into what is called a blank, which is a screw without threads. These machines produce as many as 250 per minute with, theoretically, no scrap at all, and the parts themselves are much stronger than if they had been screw machined on a lathe. The trade-off is that with screw machining, you can hold very tight tolerances, while in the case of cold heading, they have to be much looser. Cold heading is a commercial business. Parts are mass-produced in an effort to keep cost down while making the parts functional.

I have only worked for companies that were cold headers; that is the term used to describe fastener manufacturers. But each one of them made vastly different products within the cold heading range. This was demand driven and not by design, such as you would have with a washer company or a socket house that predetermines their products. My first employer was a pretty generic cold header, but they liked to make parts out of nonferrous material due to costs; the parts were value added. I am assuming that the reader understands that stainless steel, brass, and aluminum are all a lot more expensive than steel.

They made two aggressive changes after I left. One was making a new patented plastic application screw, invented by one of their old buddies; they agreed to sign a contract to distribute a line of special rivets (rivets are not usually made by cold heading companies, even though they are made on cold heading machines). The company I worked for didn't like to make anything out of stainless. Their theory was that the liability of making a mistake in production and running scrap in stainless or brass versus making the same mistake running carbon steel was too great to risk. The company I spent nearly nine years working for specialized in sems (this is short for "assembly" of a screw with a captivated washer). To further explain, the washer was very special. The ID, or inside diameter, of the washer had to be larger than the blank, or unthreaded part and smaller than the OD, or outside diameter of the threads. The washer was assembled prior to the thread rolling process, thus capturing it on the screw.

This is for ease of assembly by the OEM. He doesn't have to put the washer on the screw and then install it. It is already on the screw. We were one of the only companies making sems back then and by far the largest. The other difference was that we sold to distributors, where this was actually forbidden at the first company where I worked. They thought distributors were the enemy. In the beginning, we were also the best source of supply to the distributor for Phillips drive screws and were also known as the best source of Phillips parts for distributors.

Now, getting back to me being out of a job after working for almost nine years at one company and feeling rather lost.

I stopped at my new friend's company in Elk Grove Village. Remember the little guy who saved a dinner dance by entertaining us with the Jimmy Durante impersonator? He worked at my friend's company. He and I became friends when I worked at my first job. We seldom bought socket screws, but the machines we used were put together in socket screws, and whenever one broke, I would call him, and he'd usually just get me what I needed for free. He had a wonderful phone voice, which made him a really good inside salesperson. I think I described him as being short, thus he was given the nickname of "Munchkin." We could be cruel.

As I said I stopped there on my way home, I decided to stop in and ask my friend for some advice. Their main customers were also distributors, so I thought he might have some suggestions. He thought I should talk to Gemini Industries, one of my old employer's main competitors. This would put me about six or seven miles from home, where I had been driving thirty-two miles one way. This really did make a lot of sense.

He explained that he had grown up with Gemini's owner. They both had lived in one of the "neighborhoods".

he called his old friend on my behalf. His friend asked me to be there the next morning for an interview.

Another old friend who was an inside salesman at thea first company I worked for now owned his own company. He was now specializing in semi-tubular rivets. He had worked for another fastener company, and I called him for suggestions too. He told me I should contact them as well. He called his old boss on my behalf and got me an interview with them that very same evening.

Within a day of being devastated by leaving a job I had grown to love, I had two interviews.

This is a very small industry, where everybody knows everybody. And, as I said, if you are known to be good at your job, there is security within the business. I was still upset but beginning to feel that everything would work out.

I went off to the first of my two interviews, at Best Co. I arrived later in the afternoon and spent nearly two hours with the owner's son. He seemed very nice; he gave me the plant tour, and we talked about what I had been doing and where Best was heading. He ended the meeting by promising to call me the next day. That didn't quite happen; his call came two and a half years later. But I'll cover that later.

The following morning, I showed up bright and early at Gemini for my interview. It went very well, and I was offered a sales position at the same wage I had been making. There was no management involved, and for the time being, that was fine with me. Middle management is a most difficult job. You have to keep the "suits" happy. But you have to keep the people who work under you happy as well. It is hard to determine which is more important, because they both can be your downfall. For the time being, I was happy just to try to get sales orders and make money for the company and make a home for myself, so I could take care of my family, which was growing.

Our two little girls were born while I was at my second job, Beth in December of 1978 and Lisa in February of 1981. My priorities were changing. What I needed from a career was changing. I had no visions of grandeur. I had mouths to feed, and risk-taking was out of the picture. At least I thought so at the time.

CHAPTER 8

REPS, WAREHOUSES, ASSOCIATIONS, AND CUSTOMERS

At this point in the story, I need to go back and tie up a couple of loose ends. Aside from factories and warehouses, management and salespeople, nuts and screwballs (sorry about that), I need to cover some other interesting events and people.

About that bad joke: There are plenty of fastener industry-related jokes. If someone asks what you do for a living, and you say you're in fastener sales, they usually think you sell zippers or snaps. So you explain that you sell screws, but they get the wrong idea, and you explain that you sell screws, nuts, and bolts. People who are not in the industry have no idea what goes into making a screw or a nut. There is a company in our industry whose name is Uneeda Screw, another firm has a statue in front of its building that shows a woman shaped like a bolt running away from a man shaped like a nut, with an inscription that reads, "Not without a washer." There is an advertisement that depicts two little frogs mating, and the ad reads, "Everyone needs a little screw" (it's an ad for a miniature screw company). I titled this book, *Everyone Needs a Screw*. In fact, they are used by all of us at one time or another. They are taken for granted and are really pretty cheap, even if you have to go to the hardware store to buy what you need.

It's a small industry. But for the most part, they are very much a commercial product. OEMs now consider them "C" items. That is in comparison to "A" or "B" items. They are considered commodities. The percentage of the cost of the fasteners in a product versus the cost of the item is a pittance. Fasteners are the cheapest thing that goes into a product. But I promise you, if something goes wrong, if they are late, if a part fails, if a part is misused or misengineered, then this C item jumps to an A item in a heartbeat. Fasteners hold everything together, and they have gotten cheaper and cheaper over the years. They have been cheapened, imported, and prostituted by our own people, and while everything else increases in price, fasteners get cheaper. As I said earlier, it is a dying industry, and it is in very bad shape. Friendly competition is now panic, and they are sold by companies and salesman that have no balls.

Getting off my high horse and back to my story, there are a number of ways to sell your product. One is over the phone, another is through advertising, another is with direct salespeople, and another is through a sales representative. This is an independent, self-employed agent who owns his own agency, works on commission basis, and usually covers a set territory. Their business is often larger than yours, yet the owners or the principals they represent think they can dictate to them, demand call reports, and even tell them where to go and when. This type of relationship between a principle and a rep does not last long. Few owners of fastener companies understand how a rep works. Reps work on commission, and if 30 percent of their income comes from one company, they will get approximately 30 percent of his time, and so on.

If you are the new kid on the block, in other words a new line for him, he will invest some extra time and effort into your line. If he sees success, you will continue to get more and more, until there is a feedback effect, or it begins to level off. If he sees little success, you will not get much. You may think the company you work for is the best thing since sliced bread, but your percentage of his business may not mean much. To get more of his time, you ply him with ways to make more money, by selling your line instead of one of his other lines. This can be done by expanding your product line, giving him more things to push. You might offer sales incentives, but you need something to spark his interest.

He will give your new product or idea a chance, but it won't be for very long if it causes him to take time away from a better line that makes him more money. Sales reps are a dime a dozen, and there are twenty lousy ones for every good one. There are reps who collect lines and never work them, and there are agencies that limit how many lines they can handle and how well they fit with the other lines they represent. These are, of course, the good ones. If he is knowledgeable about your industry, then all the better.

Over the years, I have worked with my share of bad ones. But I have also been lucky enough to have been associated with some really good ones as well. They are often strange birds. It really helps if you know how reps think. They are usually hyper, and while they seem to be upbeat and positive with customers, they are usually negative and pessimistic with you. They are always thinking they are going to lose a line. But this feeling comes from experience. In the rep business, if you don't do a good job and increase sales within a territory, you are going to lose the line. But don't do too good a job, or you will be replaced with a full-time salesman. It is a fine line they walk.

Every company I've ever worked for has had management that felt these reps worked for them and they could dictate to them. Legally speaking, if you try to do this, you have to pay them as if they were employees, and not agents. I try to understand their position whenever I deal with them. Good ones can open doors for you. They have contacts with customers that they have been selling other lines to that will get you an audience with the buyer. They will always work as an agent in the field for you once the account is opened.

When you consider customers, you have to realize that purchasing is way down the food chain. I will remind the reader what my wonderful first boss said: "Real profit is made in the Purchasing Department." But generally speaking, when you are dealing with a purchasing agent who buys fasteners (you know, C items), you usually have two types of people. One is the loser who has been stuck in the same position for years and isn't going anywhere. He knows everything there is to know about fasteners and can't be told anything; there is never anything new. He has a fastener handbook he got from Reed and Prince in 1945, and it is the final authority. Of course, Reed and Prince had been out of business for many years, and there have been three editions of the *Fastener Standards* published since then. But he knows it all.

The other are young go-getters who are upwardly mobile and don't want to be bothered with knowing anything about what they are buying, because they have a computer printout with part numbers that tell them all they need to know. Now in today's market, you never get hold of them to make an appointment, because they have voice mail and never have to answer their phone. This is one reason it is so much easier to sell to distributors, because they need suppliers, while many OEMs think they don't need any more vendors, especially for a commodity item. They simply do not understand how necessary and important they can be.

One of the largest territories we had for distributor sales was the West Coast. This is obvious because of Silicon Valley and all the light manufacturing done in California. There was a movement to open our first warehouse. It was discussed at length. What to put in it? Who was to run it? I felt that if it was run properly, it could be a great idea. If it wasn't, it could be a license to steal.

A gentleman I'll call Monty had been an employee of one of our good customers here in Chicago for many years. He was chosen to open and man this new warehouse! He was an older fellow who was moving to California because his wife wanted to see movie stars (I personally can't think of a better reason to move to California). She eventually got to see some too. The only time I socialized with her was when I took her and Monty to dinner at the LA Playboy Club. I was not impressed with the place, but she thought she might see some movie stars there. We didn't. But I found out that she was afraid of escalators? We had parked in an underground parking garage, and there was an escalator going from the parking level to the lobby of the building we were under. She refused to use it. She said they were too dangerous. I asked her how that is possible. After all, if it stops, you merely walk off it. But she was content to use the (much safer) elevator.

We transferred a representative inventory after finding a small but centrally located facility. Monty hired two people to work there; one was an ultra-religious young man I'll call Gus, who read the Bible during his lunch. Nice guy but a little over the top for me. But he was a good employee and ended up working for us at another warehouse. Monty also hired a receptionist, and this blonde was a knockout. You know the blonde jokes that went around a while ago? She was the source of most of them. She was kept busy doing all the essential office duties. I arrived one afternoon, and she had a television on her desk, and she was doing needlepoint. Monty liked to fish. He bought a boat. Where did he store it? In the warehouse. I'm not sure if it was ever put to sea. It was in terrible shape; he worked on it in his spare time. As you can see, this was a booming place.

The Los Angeles Fastener Association (LAFA) was a very large and well-attended association. Our reps in LA were very active in it, but they couldn't get Monty to attend any of the monthly meetings. I argued, to no avail, that he had to go and be as active as possible. These were our customers, after all, and we got a lot of our business based on friendships formed through these organizations and their functions. But Monty was an old friend of our president; therefore, my arguments fell on deaf ears.

As I said, sales representatives can be a strange breed. They are always a little hyper and look over their shoulders, expecting to be replaced. Reps usually want a territory, but in most instances, they don't cover a territory; they cover a couple of accounts. This way, they can make a good commission and only have to call on a couple of accounts and get credit for everything sold into a territory. I don't mean to sound critical because, heck, I don't like to work very hard either, but I've never taken credit for something I had nothing to do with.

The agency we had in California was a good group. They were well known by our customers and were very active in the LAFA. I was making a sales call with one of them, a very nervous man. We were calling on an already good customer, and the owner was one of the old guard from the Midwest. All these guys had worked together way back years before. We had already made our call on the PA. As we walked down a hallway toward the exit, I noticed a nameplate above a door. I recognized the name.

As we passed it, I said to my rep, "I've got to say hello."

He grabbed my arm and whispered, "No, no, we need to speak to the receptionist first and ask permission."

I pulled away from him, stuck my head in his office, and said, "It looks like they'll let anybody out of Chicago."

He said, "Get in here."

We began to talk about all his old buddies back home in Chicago. He asked me what I knew about all of them. While all this was going on, my nervous, fidgety rep was cowering in the corner. I was afraid he was going to pass out. In the course of our discussion, our customer asked me if I could supply a part. I said I thought we could. He wanted 500m at once. I said I was sure we could do that. I called the office, got our president on the phone, and wrapped up a very nice order. It was shipped the following day. Why did I act so boldly? This was an old Chicago guy. I knew he would be tickled to talk about the old days. What could he really do? Throw us out? Nah. Would we have gotten this really nice order if I hadn't done what I did? Maybe not. Now, did my poor rep survive? He nearly didn't. He could have used an oxygen bottle in the car. Salesmen all have different methods for selling. Mine was always open, frank, and honest. It usually worked for me.

I will give you a couple of examples of things I have done with reps.

Years ago, there was a function in New York City that I attended every year for five consecutive years. It was a stag party that was held at one of the large hotels. If you readers think hard you know what a stag party is. The first time I went to it was also the first time I had ever been to New York. I had heard rumors about this event, but you know about rumors. Frankly, I believed about half of the stories. My sales rep, his employee, and one of our good customers were going together and had reserved a table next to the runway.

I'll call the customer Jesse. Let me tell you about Jesse. He is a dyed-in-the-wool New Yorker, through and through. His heavy Brooklyn accent comes across over the phone as really hard. One day, he was working on an order with one of the inside salesmen in my department. This was the guy I had offended by being too blunt with. He was rather sensitive. Well, he came into my office, complaining about Jessie. He said he just couldn't deal with him. He was on another line, so I agreed to take the call. I knew Jessie; he was no less tough on me. I tried to, diplomatically, solve whatever the problem was (I long ago forgot what it was about). Jessie was having none of it. The conversation digressed into a shouting match.

The whole day had been a particularly bad one for me and I lost it. In fact, I lost it worse than I ever did with a customer. I screamed into the phone that I was not only not going to take this order from him, in fact I wouldn't take any orders from him. I yelled that I was going to instruct everyone in my department to not accept any orders from Jessie or his company. I must confess that I did use a few four-letter words, which I never did before or since.

In the midst of my tirade, Jessie started to laugh. Do you have any idea what that does to your level of anger? It blew all the wind out of my sails. I was totally confused.

Jessie said, "Stevie, Stevie, Stevie, you just don't get it."

I said, "Get what?"

He replied, "It's only a game. Don't you understand, it's only a f—king game."

This really blew the wind out of my sails. Jessie and I have been friends now for many years. He taught me how to sell in New York City. You would think that our reps would do that, but it took a customer to explain how to deal with the New York buyers. Out of all the areas of the country we sold in, my favorite was the metropolitan New York area. They love to bust balls. That is just the New York way. While, in fact, they are an easy sell at the same time. As Jessie told me, it's a game.

Getting back to my story about this stag thing. I was on the phone with Jessie one day and told him I was planning my first trip to New York and going to this bash.

He asked me, "You've never been to it?"

I told him that I hadn't.

He said, "You won't like it." He then asked me, "Have you ever been to New York?"

Again, I told him no, I hadn't ever been there.

He replied again, "You won't like New York, either."

In fact, a few years earlier, Jessie had gone to this show and got into a fistfight; the guy he beat up went to the hospital, and my rep hid him in the men's toilet until the police left. As Jessie was telling me the story, he still believed the guy deserved it. These are tough people.

On our way to the hotel, which was across the street from Madison Square Garden, we got stopped in traffic by a bag lady who had jaywalked into the middle of a busy intersection and decided she needed to answer the call of nature; she proceeded to relieve herself right there. She stopped traffic in all four directions. There was a mounted policeman there, but all he could do was scratch his head. He just didn't know what to do.

I was sitting in the front seat as we drove through downtown New York City. As we were sitting at another light, a very well-dressed man with a neatly trimmed beard, wearing a three-piece suit, walked across the intersection in front of our car, sucking his thumb.

As we all stared at him, my rep said, "See him? He used to be a manufacturer's rep."

I am not kidding you, this was on the same car ride through New York City. After we left the car in a nearby parking garage, we had to walk only a couple of blocks to the hotel, but as we walked past Madison Square Garden, a street person, evidently feeling pretty good after drinking his paper bag lunch, fell down the steps in front on us and split his head open. Later that night, on the way back to the car, we had to walk around the people sleeping on the sidewalk. But all this was nothing to what happened inside the Statler Hotel that night.

Now, I stated earlier, Jessie had warned me that I not only was not going to like this stag thing, but I wouldn't like New York, either. I had heard many stories about this stag party. I had wondered how it could be possible for a large group of professional men could get together and make fools out of themselves the way I heard they did at this function. Burlesque, strippers, striptease, girlie shows, lap dancers: None of them hold a candle to what these ladies did. I am not a prude, not in any way, but I was really embarrassed. Here were about five hundred men all in similar businesses. Some of them were suppliers or customers of other men in the same room, and they were making absolute fools of themselves. My rep jokingly said he had brought a .45 caliber automatic with him and that if he got so drunk that he got up on the stage with one of those women, we were to please shoot him because he didn't want to face anyone when he sobered up.

The first year I went to this thing willingly, merely out of curiosity; the next four years, I was told I had to attend. That first year, my rep got up from the table midway through one of the performances and snuck over near the stage where the girls exited. As one of them was leaving the stage, he asked her to help him play a trick on us at the table, and she agreed, for fifty dollars. He picked her up and carried her, like a baby, over to the table, laid her in the middle of it, and said, "Here's dessert." She was dressed in her birthday suit. Yes, completely naked. What went on up on the stage was, well, I'll leave it up to your imagination. I always knew I worked in a low-class industry, but I had no idea how far down it really went.

That same night, I saw, for the second time in my life, the largest man I have ever seen. The first time I met Big Jerry was a few years earlier, when I was the purchasing agent at my first company. I was working hard at my desk when the receptionist called me on the intercom and said I had a visitor. Today, you have to make an appointment to get an audience with a buyer, but not back then. I told her I was busy and really couldn't see anyone. She insisted, saying I really needed to see this guy. I asked her why, but she either wouldn't or couldn't explain, just saying I had to come up front and see him.

The front lobby was more like a large closet. It was very small. The window into the office was over the receptionist's desk, and the approach to the door was from the side, so I couldn't see who was there until I actually opened the door and went out into the lobby. When I opened the door, I discovered there was not room for me and him in the lobby at the same time. Big Jerry was about six foot five and weighed at least five hundred pounds. He had a full beard, was wearing a huge ten-gallon hat, and was smoking the biggest cigar I had ever seen in my life. He also wore cowboy boots. Talk about an imposing figure. I didn't know if he was going to solicit my business or eat me.

That night in New York, he had two rooms and also hired a young lady to occupy each of them, and then he proceeded to hand out the keys to his better customers (I was not one of his better customers, thank goodness). I heard later that one of these customers blew the whistle on them, and some of New York's finest along with the house detective paid a visit to the room while they were engaged in … whatever it was they were doing.

A year later, in another function, in an effort to escape the festivities of the evening, a group of us escaped and ended up having drinks in Big Jerry's room. I asked him about getting raided the year before. He replied that he didn't get raided; it was his customer (I am omitting that person's name for obvious reasons).

You readers might think that Big Jerry was some kind of a buffoon or a joke. You would be so wrong. He was the president of a huge company and very, very sharp. The interesting thing is that the company I worked for was not one of his customers. At this time, I was traveling all over the country to these fastener conventions. He constantly went out of his way to be nice to me whenever we ran into each other at a fastener show or convention. He would introduce me to owners as well as purchasing agents and tell them to give me their business.

My wife and I had just found out she was pregnant before we went to a convention in Cyprus Gardens, Florida. When I ran into Big Jerry at the first morning meeting, I told him Jan was expecting. He made a fuss over her not only there but a month later at Grossinger's, in upstate New York. Grossinger's is a very large Jewish resort. They are kosher, and the big meal is on Friday, before sunset, of course. They only served prepared foods on Saturday, their Sabbath. At the Friday evening dinner, we were seated at a table about as far away from the entrance as you could be. Jerry had arrived late and made his grand entrance, wearing a snow-white leisure suit and a royal blue satin shirt, unbuttoned to just above his navel; he was wearing his ten-gallon hat and a maniacal chain that hung almost down to his knees. He walked through the dining room, saying hello to everyone along the way, until he spotted my lovely, beaming wife, and he made a big deal out of telling everyone in the room that she was going to have a baby. He was really something. He gave Jan a big kiss as he introduced her to everyone. There was no advantage for him to be nice like this to me. There was no way I could help him or his company.

He was a very bright and influential man in our industry. He was without a doubt the most recognizable and famous person to ever work in this goofy industry. He passed away a few years ago. I feel honored to have known him.

We had become members of all these fastener associations around the country, for sales reasons, of course. We also hired sales reps in these same areas. There was no need to have sales reps locally. But there are areas in the country where you simply must have local representation. Some areas are very clannish. Customers in these areas want to feel they have a friend, a local person who is going to go to bat for them if the need arises.

Two of these areas are New England and the Southeast. In Texas, it was impossible to make any headway without a local guy. The same way with the Southeast. Maybe they thought we were all gangsters. You know, like Al Capone or Machine Gun Kelly. Why not? Most of the people in New York think we are still fighting the Indian wars.

I once told a New York customer that I grew up in Iowa. He thought that was over near Ohio. Just outside New York, there is a place called the United States.

I had a really good rep in Texas. He was a good old salesman. He knew everybody in the industry. Everyone liked him, and he was very helpful in getting us new customers in the area. His wife was very much a part of his agency and was a delight. They were very helpful in teaching us how to deal with Texans. Until I was pulled into a meeting with the suits, and they told me they wanted OEM business in Texas. I mentioned earlier that it is hard to walk both sides of the street; by that, I mean to sell both OEM and to distributors. I said we had two very separate and distinct sales departments, and they were too busy and had no interest in knowing what we were selling to our customers.

There were some distributor customers that were doubtful as to how honest we were in telling them that the two sales departments were completely separate from one another and were often actually in competition with each other. It was always a help to have a sales rep they knew and trusted. The problem here was our guy in Texas only called on distributors. All the lines he represented were suppliers to the distributors. He had two problems. One, he didn't have any OEM contacts. The other was that if he was discovered calling on an OEM that was a customer of one of his distributor accounts, his credibility would be destroyed, and he would be jeopardizing the other lines he represented.

He and I had long talks about it, and I pleaded with him to find a way to throw something to the OEM Department, but to no avail. I told him that if he didn't do something, we would eventually hire an OEM rep in the territory. He didn't, and they did. As soon as the word got out, he called me and resigned the line. I begged him not to, but he claimed we would lose all our distributor business as soon as they knew we were actively soliciting OEM business in the territory. I told him I had very little faith in our OEM Sales Department. I didn't think they knew how to sell in Texas, and the OEM buyers wouldn't abandon their local buddies, anyway. He doubted me and resigned the line. I told him I thought he was cutting off his nose to spite his face, but we agreed to part company.

We had been able to pick up some good small accounts in Texas and one really good one outside of the Metroplex (metropolitan Dallas). The home office was in Dallas, but their branch office was eighty miles away. The branch office gave us all our orders. They had contracts with two big OEMs. The manager of this branch office became a wonderful customer and a really good friend. He was a great guy. He has been a friend now for over twenty-five years. We didn't need a rep to call on them, but we had dozens where we really needed that local area contact.

I will tell you a little secret: The very best way to find a good rep is to have your customers recommend them. I got a call from a good customer in the Metroplex area. This was a large fastener distributor company we had been selling for years. The owner's son was my usual contact. He said he heard our rep in the area had resigned and then asked me if we were going to replace him. I said yes we were, but he had to be a special guy, someone everybody down there knew and loved, and I didn't know who that might be. I asked if he had any suggestions, and sure enough, he did. The guy he suggested had worked for a local distributor. He had tried opening his own company, but it did not work out. He then was trying to become a sales rep but was struggling to get lines. He was recommended as a very well-liked guy, very knowledgeable; he felt he would be a good fit.

I learned that he was married and had two little girls, just like me, so we had something in common. I was a little tentative about hiring a rep who was not already established in his business. My customer tried to reassure me that he was well liked, and he thought he would do a good job for us and we would be happy with him. He and I hit it off at once, both professionally and personally.

Whenever I went to Texas, we worked in the Metroplex area, but we had to make two calls for sure. We had to make a courtesy call to the home office of our best customer. The owner was a complete nut. We never got a dime of business from the home office. He took great joy in harassing me that I worked for a Jewish company. Actually, that was not true. We were part of a publicly owned group of companies. But, whenever I called on him, he would come to the door wearing a yarmulke; he said he did it to make me feel at home. He called me one day back in the early 1980s to tell me to take all my savings and sell all my stock and invest it in gold. If you remember, back in the late 1970s, the price of gold was skyrocketing. I told him that all I had in stock was flour, sugar, and canned goods. He was very serious, though. He made an absolute fortune. I was told that he actually sold his company and bought gold. I was discussing beer with him one day. He asked me if I liked Coors Beer. At that time, it was not sold east of the Missouri River. I told him that we folks in Chicago couldn't buy it. So he sent me a case via UPS.

There was a little plane that made a run to the town our customer was in. I stopped taking that little commuter flight when we got put onto a holding pattern because of a cow on the runway. But I'd usually call the buyer/manager and tell him what day to expect us and then call him later to settle on a time. It's always nice to have lunch with your good customers, especially when they are friends as well as customers. I called him and said we planned on being there around 11:30 a.m.

He said, "No, that's too late." I asked him why, and he said, "I have a guide set up for noon. We are going fishing, aren't we?"

He already knew how much I liked to fish. They do a lot of large-mouth bass fishing in that part of the country.

On one of my sales/fishing trips, he decided we would just go out in his boat. There are two lakes close by, both of which have good bass fishing. We started fishing in the early evening, and it was getting later and later. We were having a great time. We had caught some fish but nothing to brag about. But as the sun was going down, he remembered he didn't have running lights on his boat, and since we were about thirty minutes away from the dock, and the sun had gone below the horizon about twenty minutes earlier, it was going to get really close to not making it in before complete darkness. We quickly pulled in our lines and got set up for running. A bass boat can really fly across the water, and we were going full speed. I began to wonder if we were going to get there before complete darkness set in when we hit a sandbar going about sixty miles per hour. The motor flew up over the transom and made a nasty whirring sound. The boat skidded sideways and came to very abrupt stop.

We were both rather startled. I was sitting in the middle of the boat on the left side next to my guide, who was driving. Neither one of us said anything for a moment.

I turned to him questioningly, and he said, very calmly, "Damn, I went over that spot last week."

The boat was sitting on what I thought was a solid sandbar in the middle of the lake. It was almost pitch-black at this time. Now, keep in mind that in those days, when you make a sales call, you wear a coat and tie. Before we left to go fishing, I took off the tie, and he had given me a light windbreaker to wear. But I still was wearing dress pants and dress shoes. Here we sat in the middle of a lake, nearly pitch-black. Wait, it gets better.

He turned to me and said, "It is a shame about those pants."

I realized we were going to have to get out of the boat and somehow physically move the heavy bass boat off the sandbar and into deeper water.

I look down at my trousers and said, "No problem; I'll just take them off."

So, off came the shoes and socks, pants, and jacket. We were just about to slip over the side and start pushing when the lake flies hit us. They were in the midst of their annual hatch, and they descended on us by the millions. My white shirt was almost black with them. They went into our mouths, ears, eyes, and noses. I have never eaten so many bugs at one time, before or since.

Fighting the bugs, the dark, almost naked, I slipped into the water, thinking we were on a foot or so of water and solid sand. Well, I was wrong; it was quicksand. I sunk up to my chest, and the only thing that kept me from going completely under was the fact that I was holding on to the side of the boat. There was nothing under our feet at all. I sort of bounced up and down until my foot hit the limb of an old dead tree that was in the sand. This gave me some footing.

At this point we had to decide which way to push the boat. The closest way was behind us, where we had entered, but to push a boat backwards that had the outboard motor jammed into the sand was impossible. We agreed to continue in the direction we were headed, hoping the water above the sand might get a little deeper. We started a combination of lifting and sliding the boat ahead while trying to find footing in quicksand and fighting lake flies, all at the same time. It seemed like hours, but in actuality, it probably was only a few minutes we were in deep enough water for the motor to operate. We jumped in and took off, laughing all the way to the dock, and we still get a chuckle out of it today. It very well could have been a serious situation, but it was so funny at the time. Guys just don't consider how bad it could have been.

CHAPTER 9

GETTING ON WITH MOVING ON

It's time to get back to my story. I had been offered a new job at Gemini and accepted it. One really good thing: It was so much closer to home. I did not expect a call from Best, the company I met with the previous evening. I was waiting for them to call, but they never did. This job seemed like a natural fit. Most of my customers at my previous company told us that Gemini was our main competition. The difference was that Gemini did not carry inventory. Sems, that is the assembly of a washer on the screw, was one of their main products. Best did not like selling parts to distributors, although they did sell to a few.

I've indicated the most domestic manufacturers considered fastener distributor companies to be competition, and why should they sell to their competition? That attitude has done a complete reversal in recent years, mainly because of how the OEMs want their fasteners shipped to them. It used to be that you made a part and shipped it. At the very most, there would be monthly shipments. In recent years, the Just in Time (JIT) theory came into use, and parts had to be made and then stored and doled out in small amounts, sometimes every other day. Another system that had begun was bin stocking. This is where the supplier is actually in the factory and fills the bins on the line where the parts are installed. Yet another is called con-bon. This is where the customer's parts are in a bonded area. They pay for the parts that are removed and put on the production line. The removal triggers a replacement on the part of the supplier. Fastener manufacturers are not usually equipped to provide this kind of service, while distributors often were.

I am now working for my third employer. I made to believe Gemini was my biggest competitor for the past nine years. I was wrong. Our shared customers had been lying to us. We both had been cutting our prices to compete for orders that we, in fact, were not really competing for. I'll explain. Both companies did make the same products, and they both liked selling distributors. But my previous employer made mostly smaller parts, while Gemini made larger parts. No one ever seemed to understand that at either company. Somehow, maybe since I had worked at both places, I figured it out. The theory at both companies was explained thus. One wanted numbers of parts out the door, and the other based success on tonnage. I really concentrated on this idea. I guess I did have a certain amount of success; two and half years later I was awarded a plaque for the salesman of the year.

You might think this meant that everything went smoothly. Oh, my, would you be wrong. I felt I had been mistreated by my two previous employers, and I promised myself I would not allow that to happen again. Unfortunately, right off the bat, it started. The sales manager, who I'll call Ted, was rather short in stature. His boss was a very professional woman I had known for years. I had a lot of respect for her.

Ted and I did not get along from the very start. In all honesty, I did go out of my way to terrorize him. As I said, he's rather short and has a personal problem with this. No one else would, if he himself ignored it, but he kept it out in front of himself all the time so you couldn't help but make it part of the relationship.

Gemini was very structured in how they sold their parts. Everywhere I had worked prior to this, salespeople were instructed on the pricing system and given a minimum price level. But whatever you could get over that was 100 percent pure profit. Not here; you had to sell according to their setup. I've been told I have a problem with authority figures, and that may be a little bit true. I feel I do lose respect for those in authority when they don't deserve it. I may be wrong, but authority is something that should be earned, not required. I think back to my first boss. He was the best. I loved and feared him. Since then, no one was able to measure up. Certainly not my new one. I'll give you an example.

I had been working there about a week. I was walking through the office, and as I passed the VP's desk, I told her a joke. I don't remember the joke, but it was clean. She laughed; I laughed.

As I returned to my desk. Ted walked up to me and said, "Excuse me, we're here to get orders, not tell jokes."

I replied, "Oh, well, I tell you, Ted. I'm going to be spending one-third of my life here, and I'm going to enjoy myself, despite you."

As you can imagine, that was the start of a long and loving friendship.

Salespeople at Gemini were given a huge stack of costing information. Every page in every section was exactly the same as everyone else's. When these sheets were updated, it was a very formal process, with Ted standing over you to watch you put it in, and you had to hand him the one you removed (he would take it away to some hiding place somewhere).

We were actually given periodic tests in pricing, and your sale price had to be the same as everyone else's, to the penny. I suppose that the theory behind this was good for them, but I never sold that way. Gemini took pride in never hiring anyone who had ever worked for another fastener company. This way, they could train new people properly, in the Gemini way, so they wouldn't have any bad habits that might have been learned from another company. Again, I felt this was dumb because when salespeople, who are on the firing line, know something and can get more money, this extra money is pure profit. I think I was the first person hired in the Sales Department who had worked for another fastener company.

Their pricing system had flaws. I'll give you one example: I had taken an inquiry from a distributor customer on a very long part. As I worked up the price using the given setup, it seemed like it was way too cheap. So before I quoted the setup price, I went back to using pricing systems we used at my previous employer. The price I came up with was eight dollars a thousand higher than the Gemini setup. I quoted the part my way and got the order immediately, indicating to me that even my price may have been too cheap as well. I went to Ted and said I got an order, but I didn't use the company pricing.

He said, "Oh, gee, what'd you do?"

I asked Ted what the price on this part should be. He was such negative person, he replied that I should know how to price it. I said I did but wanted him to verify my numbers. He worked it up using our system and came up with the same lower price I had. I told him I had gotten the order at a higher price. I handed him my order and showed him how much I got for it and told him at the same time that his pricing method, at least for this product, was wrong.

They immediately changed the setup. Was Steven given any credit for pointing out their error, which had cost them a lot of money and would make them a lot more profit in the future? What do you think?

Now, it seems to me that if you hire people with experience, you might be able to learn what other companies do. They are in business too, so they must be doing something right. They might, in fact, do some things better than you do.

Just because I didn't have any respect for Ted doesn't mean I didn't have respect for other people at Gemini. Jane, the owner's niece, was the VP of sales. She's very bright and was well trained; she handled customers well and was very gentle when dealing with people who worked under her.

But Ted, who I said had a serious Napoleon problem, was another story. The inside salespeople were required to fill out daily call reports and had to list at least twenty cold calls a day. They were even provided with a written sales pitch to use. I can't do that and never did. I would turn in two or maybe three a day. I generated more sales than anyone else without doing this. I thought it was a waste of time and felt it might be a good way to sell vinyl siding but not fasteners. Ted had taken a Dale Carnegie sales course and knew this was the best way to sell. He was somewhat upset that I was not making the required number of calls or, at least, was not recording them. He called me into a vacant office for a meeting one day.

He had taken about three months of these call reports and spread them all over the top of the desk, in chronological order, and said to me, "You know you are supposed to be making at least twenty calls a day." I said I knew that. He continued, "But you are only turning in two or three. You are on the phone all day, every day. We just want to know who you are talking to."

I told him those were personal calls. He sat there for a moment and then said, "No, they're not." I knew he knew that because he would listen in on everyone's phone conversations.

I said to him, "Look, Ted, I know what you are getting at, but is there something wrong with my sales?"

He sheepishly said no, there wasn't, and in fact, I had more business than any other salesperson there. But, as he said, "they just wanted to know who I was talking to." I told him I completely understood where he was coming from, but I am basically very lazy. I don't like to work very hard, and if I can book orders without working hard, I'd prefer that to working my butt and achieving fewer results. I never like to waste time. A few good calls are better than dozens worthless ones.

Then I said to him, "Look, Ted, if my sales drop, you have every right to make demands of me, but as long as my sales numbers are good, why don't you leave me alone?"

Another time, he called me into the same vacant office and asked me what we had to do to work closer together. This was totally out of character for him, and I assumed someone put him up to it. I asked him what he meant by that, and he explained that I had been with Gemini for over two years, and we had never gotten along very well. He wanted to know if I had any answer for it.

I said to him, "Well, I think that I am awfully sensitive, and my feelings get hurt easily, and I hold these feelings in, which is not a very healthy thing to do, and I know it. I tend to blow situations up much larger than they really are, and there is no place for that while trying to do the pressure-filled job of sales. But on the other hand, you should work on not being such an asshole."

Well, he was taken aback by this, to say the least. He wanted to know what I meant.

I replied, "Look Ted if someone comes in on Monday morning and asks how your weekend was, you get angry."

He said, "You're damn right. That's an invasion of my privacy; it's none of their business." I had proved my point.

We had a saleslady there for a long time. She was older than most of us and was probably the second person who was hired who had previous industry experience. Now, she's in sales; she does pricing. She should have known some of the basics of sales. But if she did, she sure didn't have the intestinal fortitude to do it on her own. One of the rules in the office was that we were not allowed to speak to each other. (You may not believe that, but it's true.) I never understood that reasoning. But this didn't stop her; she would roll her chair over to my desk and ask me a question about pricing. Ted always got up and came over to see what was being said. This happened quite often, and it caused me to wonder what the big deal was.

One particular time, she said, "Now Steve, I know I have asked you this many times before, and I know it's a stupid question, and I promise I will never ask it again if you will please answer it just one more time."

I told her not to worry about it, and what was her problem? I added, "There are no stupid questions, only stupid answers." I asked her what she wanted to know.

She went on, "How do I take 8 percent off this price?"

You know what? She was right; it was a stupid question. Any junior high math student should be able to answer that one.

Here caome Ted looming over us like a Peruvian condor, I said to her, "Alright let's take a look at this. The price you want to discount is $17.68. I want to do this so you can understand it. What is 100 percent of $17.68?"

She said it's $17.68.

I said, "Good, now what would be one percent of $17.68?" She said that you would just move the decimal point over two places, making it $0.1768, or $0.18, rounded off. I praised her for that one. I explained that if she was to subtract $0.18 from $17.68, that would be reducing it by 1 percent. She agreed, so I told her she just had to do it seven more times. She said, "Is that all I have to do:" Ted was so pissed at me. That was because he had to approve all her pricing.

Gemini was very structured in their pricing systems. That was not the only thing they were strict about. There were combination locks on all the doors, except the ones going into the toilets (thank God for that). They all had different combinations, so you had to have the proper security clearance to go from one part of the building to another. These combinations usually did not remain secret for very long, so they get changed from time to time. This, of course, caused confusion because people were supposed to be able to go from one place to another and were usually concerned about more important things than the secret code; they found themselves asking for help to get back to their work area.

I had been working at Gemini only a few days. I was calling some of my contacts from my years of selling distributors, being careful not to step on the toes of the other salespeople. We were all assigned accounts. If you came up with a new one, it had to be in your territory. This, I felt, was also stupid. Sales is 20 percent price and 80 percent personalities. With distributor sales, especially, the first guy back with a price often gets the order, regardless of price. If you have a relationship with an account that is within someone else's territory, I thought, it was more important to get the order than to worry about feelings. After all, we were not paid any commission on sales.

But trying to keep this in mind, I started calling people they had never heard of. One was a small company up north. I'll call him Jim. When I say small, I mean small. He had three employees. He had been in the business for years, in fact, as a high school student, he worked for one of the local import companies.

Before Jim went into business for himself, he worked for a while for a distributor that was owned by a maniac. Now, this might seem harsh, but I will give you a couple of examples. He was known to slam his hand in a drawer repeatedly to make himself angrier. He had ripped phones out of the wall and thrown them out of his office. He got so angry once that he fired all his employees and sent everyone home (he called them all back the next day). Once he got angry at one of his warehouse workers, who took exception, decided to retaliate, and chased his boss all over the building. He ran into his office and locked the door. The pissed-off warehouse worker pounded on the office door. Jim showed him how he could get into the boss's office by going outside and crawling through the window. Jim also worked for a short time at one of the larger manufacturing companies.

I had my own experience with this character. I had called him for a sales appointment and set it up as a luncheon. I was very ill at ease the entire time. He was so nervous, he was actually quivering. Somehow, the conversation turned to Cabbage Patch Dolls. They were almost impossible to get at that time. My sister-in-law was shopping in a local mall when a semi-truck pulled in and started to sell them off the back of the truck. There was no limit, and she bought four or five. She gave us two, one for each of my little girls.

He had been searching for one for his little girl, but to no avail. He offered to buy one of mine and offered me two hundred dollars. I, of course, refused. They were for my little girls. If he thought for one minute I would take one from my daughters, he was sadly mistaken. When I told my wife this story, she was upset that I didn't take the offer. But these were my girls; are you kidding?

When Ted finally decided to go into business for himself, it was for a manufacturer in Wisconsin. He would open a sales facility in the suburbs, while the manufacturing plant would be in Wisconsin. They separated shortly when the plant made reject after reject. He later claimed they offered to supply hammers with their orders just so they could make the screws work.

The distribution branch of this little company was the only thing that made a profit. Any profit he made was used to cover the mistakes of the factory. When he was getting his company started, he approached me and explained that they were a very small company but assured me we would be paid promptly. Regal Fasteners became a very good customer.

Gemini had heard of this company but knew nothing about them. I told him that neither did I, really. I kept in contact with them, knowing I might be able to get some business. He gave me an opportunity and received an order worth forty-five hundred dollars. That's a nice order. I was really excited in getting started. I did all the things you need to do to process a new account and passed it on through the proper channels. The next day, all hell broke loose.

I need to interject something right now. Something happened once that you might think was humorous. I got an email from one of my customers, asking if we could put together a rush order for them to pick up tomorrow. It seems that in their haste to do their physical inventory, they mixed these two parts. A total of three boxes of each part were involved. The buyer stated that they simply did not have the time or inclination to sort them. I did a quick check, and sure enough, we had them in stock.

Now, I like orders; heck, that's my job. But one of the parts was a steel nut, while the other was a nylon washer. I wondered if they had a magnet; all they had to do was use a hand magnet to pick up the nuts, leaving the washers in the bottom of the box. It would take about two minutes. Does this seem dumb to you? First, how do you mix a nylon flat washer with a box of steel nuts? How do you do it three times? Then, why wouldn't you just use a magnet and sort them? That's why I love this business.

Getting back to my story, the next day, all hell broke loose. The bookkeeper/controller/financial person, also the owner's sister, came out of her office, waving a sheet of paper over her head like it was a flag, screaming (God, I hate working for a family-owned business).

Anyway, she was screaming, "Who took this order from this outfit, Regal Fasteners?"

Now, how do I describe her? She's not the easiest person to get along with. But regardless, I raised my hand and said I had taken the order in question. She stood over my desk and yelled, "If you think that for one minute that I am going to give forty-five hundred dollars in credit to a company that D&B says has only three employees and is only worth fifteen hundred dollars, you are sadly mistaken."

I remained calm; I didn't think it would be a good idea to challenge someone who was that mad. I asked her to give me back the order, which she still was still holding in her mitt, and I would merely call and cancel the order, telling them we couldn't do business with them.

She didn't do that; if fact, she ignored me completely and kept on yelling, as if I hadn't said anything. I tried to get her to calm down, to not get so upset, I would be happy to cancel the order. This whole thing was becoming embarrassing; everyone in the office heard the commotion and was watching us. She finally finished by saying she was going to give the order to the owner.

A few minutes later, I was summoned into the owner's office. He asked me who Regal Fasteners was, and I told him how they started and what I knew about them. Yes, it was a very small company, but they paid their bills very promptly. He then asked if my previous employer sold them and how much. I told him our annual sales with Regal was about two hundred thousand dollars.

He immediately turned to his controller, who was standing there the whole time, tapping her foot, and snapped, "Put that order through, now."

She literally stomped out of his office. All was good, until one week later, when I got another order from them for five thousand dollars. It was like an instant replay of the same performance of a week earlier. Again, I was called into the boss's office, and he asked me to promise him that Regal was good for the money. I assured him that they were, but he asked if I could set up a meeting with the owner. I told him I would set it up. That was the start of a very long, mutually beneficial relationship that lasted for the next twenty years.

Starting in the early 1980s, there has been annual national fastener shows. For twenty years, it was held in Columbus, Ohio, and then, it was moved to Las Vegas.

The routine went something like this: All the exhibitors show up on a Monday to set their booths; as soon as this was done, you either played golf or went to one of the hospitality suites sponsored by exhibitors at the various hotels in the area. Some of these were very nice. Tuesday, the show opened at 9:00 a.m. and closed at 4:00 p.m.

Tuesday was a night for either sales meetings or entertaining your distributor customers. (For obvious reasons, OEM customers were not supposed to attend. It would be stupid to bring a customer to an industry trade show; why introduce them to all of your competition?)

Wednesday, the show closed at 3:00 p.m., and exhibitors were not supposed to start breaking down their booths until then. Of course, the traffic was almost nil after noon, so by three, nearly all the booths were packed away. Then we all had to go back to overloaded desks and try to catch up. These events are very tiring, and if you ever attended one of these things or actually worked a booth, you know they are very taxing.

I went to Columbus, Ohio, for nearly twenty years in a row to either attend or work in a booth. I grew to really dislike it. After a few years, it was the same old thing. The same booths, the same people, nothing new. What it was good for was finding a supplier for a new product a customer wanted you to supply, or hiring a new rep in a territory, or for reps looking for a new line to represent. I guess that's called networking.

Gemini always had a nice booth and paid for a prime location on the floor so as to get the maximum amount of traffic. One year after the booth was set up on Monday, an old friend of mine grabbed me and said we should go a hospitality suite, have a few free drinks, and eat some nice munchies. I had known him from the time I first was given the purchasing responsibilities. He continued to be a personal friend. So off we go to a hotel down the street for the intention of some good food that was free and some well-needed alcohol. While we were there, I met the purchasing manager for one of our distributor customers. He never called us personally; that was done by people who worked under him. This particular company (his name and theirs will go unmentioned) never took a quoted price without pressuring us for a lower one. I stated earlier how strict Gemini was in their pricing setups; there was no way anyone was going to get a better price. This didn't matter, and whoever was quoted a price would press for something better. When they got nowhere with the sales person, they would then call the sales manager and then call again and pressure the VP. Not being satisfied, they would call our owner's brother. This only resulted in the original salesperson being chastised for letting it get that far. Of course, we salespeople had no control who they called when we were done with the original call. But we did go so far as to copy the quotes for this company and give one to everyone in sales, so we didn't have to waste time duplicating our work.

Now, here I am, sitting having a drink with the PA from this very same company. I thought we were having a very pleasant discussion, so I decided to approach this subject of pricing policy. I explained how rigid our pricing setup was. I agreed that his people were only trying to do their job and get the best price possible, but the whole exercise was a waste of time.

I'll give you an example of what I did once. The buyer for this company had gotten my price and gone around me time and time again, so this time, I decided to turn the tables a bit. He asked me a price on a special part. I worked up the cost and priced it according to the setup. But when I called him back to give him the price, instead of telling him what it was, I asked him what he wanted to pay. This totally confused him. He didn't know how to respond.

I said, "Let's do this differently this time. Instead of you bickering with me over the price I give you and you having to call someone else here for a better price, why don't you just tell me what you want to pay, and if we can live with it, we will."

He thought for a moment and decided this was a good idea. Little did he know that the price he wanted was higher than the price I had worked up. So I agreed to it immediately. He then wanted a better price. He didn't get it.

Back to the suite; little did I know he was drunk long before I ever sat down with him. He had to be because his reaction was very weird. He went nuts. He got abusive, vulgar, and basically out of control. I was shocked and tried to calm him down. He got up and only got louder. I was trying to remain calm, but it was really becoming embarrassing. I was able to remain calm until he got personal, not to me but to my employer. Now he was stepping over the line. He had touched a live wire.

I stood up and confronted him. One of my supplier friends tried to step between us and started to push me out into the hallway. There was an overflow of people out there, and he got even more vulgar. I was really mad at this point and wanted to punch the little shit. My friend was being much more level-headed; he knew this was going to get ugly and pushed me toward the elevator. It opened up as we got there; he pushed me in, turned around, and started pushing this asshole away from the elevator door.

I thought long and hard about what to do. I knew the guy was drunk, but there were a lot of people in that room, and they probably didn't hear the whole conversation. I didn't want the management of Gemini to get this whole event secondhand, so I went to our owner's room and told him what happened and how badly he had been dissing our company.

Now, the owner of Gemini was a big man and had a temper of his own. I had to stop him from leaving the hotel room and going back to the hospitality suite to beat the crap out of this guy. I had calmed down enough at this point to know this was not the thing to do. I explained that he must have been really drunk and to let it go. I just wanted him to hear it from me and not secondhand.

Alright, now here comes the fun part: Everything was forgotten about until ten years later. I was now actually working at Regal Fasteners (that story will come much later), and my old friend, who was still the sales manager for the same import company, was calling on me. He asked if I knew who was working at Gemini. I told him I had no idea who worked there anymore. He told me it was the same clown I had had the run-in with in Columbus so many years earlier. I told you readers that this is a very small industry, and everybody knows everybody. I thought that this might be fun. With him sitting in my office, I called the owner of Gemini on the phone. The conversation went something like this:

Me. "Good morning, how are you?
Boss. "Fine Steven, what's up?
Me. "Do you remember the incident in Columbus where that drunk PA who worked for ***** got so belligerent?"
Boss. "Yeah, I remember."
Me. "Guess what his name is? It's **********!"
Boss. (Long pause). "Well, you know, he really is a pretty good employee."
Me. "Good; just don't let him drink."

Believe it or not, this pretty good employee was gone a month later. Maybe that is mean but I still felt avenged.

I was doing pretty nice business with some customers in Tennessee, and the Southwest Fastener Association (SFA) was having their spring convention at the Opryland Hotel in Nashville. I went down there to make sales calls for a few days prior to the convention. This was the largest hotel I had ever seen. It has many bars in it, of course, including one on the main level, down the hallway leading from the front door, behind a spiral staircase.

It is small and intimate. I was supposed to meet the sales rep I had hired way back at my second job. He, being from Texas, was an active member of the SFA. (That's the Southwest Fastener Association) He met me on Thursday evening about six o'clock. I had gotten there about five thirty, and at that time, I was into margaritas, the frozen ones especially. He and I had not seen each other for some time. Remember, I had hired him, and he still had the line and was doing a very good job. He said he had set up a blind date for himself with an employee of a local Nashville distributor. He was going to take her to the Grand Old Opry radio show that airs every Saturday night. We were hammering drinks pretty hard. He was concerned that I was drinking so much tequila, and I told him I was on a quest to drink this particular bar out of it. I failed.

We went our separate ways to get showered and cleaned up for a social gathering that evening, when the phone in my room rang. He said my old friend and customer from Texas and his wife had come to the convention without a room reservation. He wanted to know if I would give them my room and move in with him. I was happy to do a favor for him and his wife, and I also knew it wouldn't hurt in getting future business.

The week was busy, tiring, and almost uneventful. Since I now had a roomie, he asked me to join him and his date and go to the Grand Ole Opry Saturday evening. Very reluctantly, I agreed. His date was very attractive, outgoing, and intelligent, and we had a nice dinner, and the show was fun. Afterwards, we ended up in the same bar he and I had met in that first evening. It was already getting pretty late; I had had plenty to drink, and since the next day was a pack-up-and-leave day, I was hoping to get some sleep. About this time, he started ordering Long Island Iced Teas. I'm sure you know what these are; you also know that if you've already been drinking and it's late, you are going to get really potted. I don't know how many he drank over the next two hours, but he was feeling no pain.

I had stopped drinking much earlier, and his date had also. It was getting very late. We just sat there and watched in amazement how he continued to drink these incredibly powerful mixed drinks.

Finally, he turned to her and said, "Well, honey, are you ready to go upstairs and get naked and make love, or not?" (By the way, he didn't say "love.")

I nearly fell out of my seat. I couldn't believe he had said that. Her reply was wonderful; she calmly looked at her watch and said, "I was ready about an hour ago, but it's a little late now."

He just looked dejected and said, "Oh damn."

I guess some lines are better than others.

One year, a month or so prior to the Columbus show, I was approached by my boss (remember the one I didn't get along with?), who called me into a private meeting and told me that the management decided to have a model in the booth to pin carnations on people who stopped by. They didn't want anyone taking time away from selling to do this, so we could hire a pretty girl to do it.

I wasn't sure what that had to do with me until I was assigned the task of hiring her. I told him I had no idea how to go about hiring a model. He said that neither did he, but they wanted me to get it done. I said I would try.

This was before the internet, so I started looking into modeling agencies in Columbus and Cincinnati. I thought one of them might have something for us to choose from. I started making the calls, asking for references, and asking for photographs of the girls. It turned out there were three modelling agencies in Columbus. There are product shows where the girls asked to be dressed very seductively, but we didn't want that at all. We wanted her to be dressed very professionally, maybe a woman's business suit or a conservative dress. I had spent a few days on this when I was called into a meeting with Jane, the VP of sales.

She sat me down and asked me what I was doing. I told her what I had been asked to do. She said she was forbidding me from going through with it because she refused to have another woman in the booth with her, especially a model. Now let me describe Jane to you. If she was overweight, had bad teeth, and was repulsive to look at, I could understand her feelings. But no, she is very attractive, very professional, very knowledgeable about the business, and extremely personable. She was, and I'm sure still is, a very attractive lady in her own right and should have had no concerns about having a model in the booth with us. But I guess I don't know women very well. Regardless, she forbade me from continuing to look for a model. I told her that the request came from management. She said she didn't care who it came from; she didn't want another woman in the booth.

Oh, boy, I knew being put in the middle of something, was going to be bad. I told my little friend that his boss told me under no uncertain terms that I was being forbidden from continuing with my search. He told me that no matter what Jane said, I had to do it.

I knew this was going to turn out bad, and I decided I better go as carefully as possible to get a young lady who wouldn't be a threat to her. I settled on an agency in Columbus that sent me photographs of various models. All of them were lovely, of course, but we finally settled on one. There was only a number attached to the picture; no names were included. I opted for a girl who looked nice. We agreed on her, and I told the agency what her duties would be and the hours she had to be there. I was quoted a price, which was reasonable, and then was told that her name was … ready? You guessed it: Jane. I don't think I have to tell you what the reaction was. Our Jane actually accused me of doing it on purpose. I tried to assure her that I hadn't, that it was just dumb luck. But I'm not sure she ever forgave me.

As it worked out, she did a nice job. She was to be there for both Tuesday and Wednesday of the show; we provided her with lunch, and she had to look nice, smile, and pin carnations on the people who stopped by the booth. The first day, the owner of Regal Fasteners (remember, by now a very valued customer) camped in our booth for half the day, sniffing around our model the whole time. He finally set up a date with her that night, in hopes of, well, you know.

As I later found out, the date went well. In fact, better than I could have hoped for. She dumped him later in the evening for another fastener Don Juan.

The next morning couldn't have turned out better. I told you readers that my boss was somewhat height challenged. Well, the owner of Regal was only about an inch taller. When the show opened on Wednesday, our model was not on time. In fact, she was quite late. My little boss was getting really upset with me, of course (like I had anything to do with it).

I told him that as far as I knew, she went out with Mr. You-Know-Who, one of our better customers.

So, in his best salesmanship manner, he approached my customer and said, "Our model hasn't shown up yet; I understand you kept her out late last night."

He responded, "Yeah, she likes taller men."

Ooh, that smarted. Six months later, at a smaller local product show, Regal's owner was able to get a shot in at our Jane. He approached our booth and jokingly said to her "Excuse me, are you the Jane I'm supposed to pick up at this show?"

She is, as I said, is a very classy lady. She responded by playfully poking him and chastising him in fun.

Unfortunately, our little friend heard all this and said to him, "Ha ha, let's just see if you get your f—king parts."

The reply was, "Ha ha, let's just see if you get your f—king money."

There was one other story (well, there really are a lot more, but they aren't quite so funny). The company had hired a number of guys who were originally from the Middle East. One of them we'll call Omar. As far as I was concerned, he was the nicest. His job was quality control. He was very knowledgeable and was also a really nice guy. I had to see him on something, not important to this story. I was told he had made an emergency trip home due to the death of his brother. Around a week later, I saw him in his office and went in to offer my condolences.

I lost my brother way back in 1967 due to a one-car accident. He had graduated from Iowa State University with a degree in architecture. He was an all-state center on our football team. He was a wonderful artist. He was six foot two with black hair and very good looking. He was driving his new Porsche convertible, on his way home from Des Moines to see his new fiancée. The whole thing was really tragic. He had the world by the tail and was really getting ready to enjoy life. There is a reason for this little aside.

So, getting back to Omar. I went into his office to offer my condolences. He thanked me, and I mentioned that I had lost my brother as well. I asked him how his brother died. He said it was an automobile accident.

I said, "I'm so sorry; my brother also died in an auto accident; it involved only one car."

He replied that so was the one involving this brother. I asked him what his brother did. He said he was an architect. Of course, so was mine. He asked if my brother was also an artist. Yes, he was. Wow! This was getting very weird. So I asked him how the accident occurred. He said that he ran into a camel. At that point, I began to lose it and left the room to keep from laughing.

I had been at Gemini for two and half years. I had made them a lot of money, opened up some major accounts, and taken a considerable amount of stress at the same time. It was about then that I got a phone call from the son of the owner of Best Co. Remember, he was going to call me the next day two and a half years before. He asked me if I could come for a second interview. I was really not very happy at Gemini and was interested in what they might be offering.

I went to Best and was introduced to Larry Jones, who was the VP of sales. He would be my immediate superior. He had been the VP of sales at a major manufacturer in Rockford for over twenty years and the president of another major company in our industry. Many years earlier, when I worked for my prior company, the lunch group I went out with often ran into him and his group. I was, frankly, not very impressed with him because he would sit at the head of their table with his group around him. It looked like the king and his court.

In weighing my pros and cons, I had been very restricted in trying sell for Gemini. Their pricing restrictions seemed silly to me. There was no room for me in management. If you want to make more money, you usually have to be in management. In fact, my salary had actually been reduced. I never understood the reason for that move. I was told they just didn't feel they had to pay me that much anymore.

What was actually said to me was, "We have a million dollars of new business. If you leave, we don't think we'll lose all of it. You can quit if you want."

I guess they expected me to quit after that move, but I couldn't. You see, I still had that family to feed. This new opportunity was another family-owned company, which could be another stressful ordeal, but I was being offered a management position as assistant to the VP. I would be working under two very respected and well-known giants in the business. I thought I could really learn a lot from them. I agreed to make the change.

There was a lot that happened between accepting the new job and actually making the move.

I had made my decision and had picked the day I would give them notice, but that very morning, Jane approached me and asked me to join her in a private meeting. This was not going to be a bad one. She just said the management had decided to have a nice dinner with all the salespeople and their spouses to celebrate a good year in sales and asked me if I had a particularly favorite restaurant. I told her that Jan and I always loved Port Edward's. This is a rather pricy seafood restaurant in Algonquin, Illinois, on the banks of the Fox River.

This was the favorite restaurant of my dear friend I rode to work with. Jan and I went there a few times with him and whoever he was dating at the time. It is a wonderful seafood restaurant that I have introduced a number of people to, and no one is disappointed.

Jane was delighted; she said she and her husband also loved it. She thought it was a good idea and said she'd run it by the owners and see if they would agree. They did, so I decided to wait until after the dinner to give my notice. This dinner was a crowning story for me and Gemini.

Before I get into the dinner, I must introduce a very good friend I'll call Gene.

Gene had started at Gemini about a year earlier. He was another salesman who had previous experience (I guess they began to change their policy). We hit it off immediately. He grew up in Iowa, was a huge Hawkeye fan, and worked for a large screw company prior to coming to Gemini. The owner was very sharp, very successful, and a bit weird.

Have you noticed there are a lot of strange people in this business? I have nothing to compare them to, so I don't know if all businesses are like this, or just the ones I ended up working for.

Monty, his old boss, was an old friend of the president of my second employer. The only thing I really regret is that I was never able to see these two together, just to see whose ego was bigger. Gene had been working on an inside sales desk and was getting screwed out of commissions that were due to him. The person doing the screwing had an inside track to the top management, and so Gene felt there was no recourse except to quit. That is how he came to be at Gemini. Gene and I both love to fish and have enjoyed a number of fishing trips, including a fly-in trip to Canada.

Men really enjoy kibitzing with each other, kidding each other, and teasing each other, and it sometimes seems to become cruel. Women, especially, don't understand how we can do and say the things we do to each other and remain friends.

Gene and I were in Canada on one of these fishing trips, and we were discussing where to go and where to fish for walleyes, or northern pike. We asked the owner of the camp if there were any muskies in the area, and he said there was a portage lake that was full of them. We got instructions on how to get to this lake and decided to go for it. We had to portage into two lakes and were told to be careful of bears in the area. We still wanted to take the chance to catch one of the most elusive, hardest fighting trophy fish in the world. They are said to be the fish of a thousand casts (or something like that). The bottom line is, they are really hard to catch. There are fishermen who actually try for muskies for years and never catch one. The opportunity seemed worth the time and possible danger to pursue.

We worked for about three hours just to get to this lake. We were instructed to go to the far side and to fish on the leeward side of a particular island. We found the spot and fished there for over half an hour, with no hits. We were just about to start trolling to see if we could find any fish that way when I got a hit. It was the most spectacular fish I've ever caught. He jumped and tail-walked four or five times before I landed it. It was of legal size but not a trophy, so we took some pictures, weighed it, and released it.

We continued fishing, hoping, of course, for a really big one. Later in the day, we were casting up against a wooded bank. I was sitting down in the middle of the boat and looking directly into the sun that was glistening off the lake, so I was basically blind to anything in the water. Gene was standing in the back of the boat, just in front of the back seat. We were drifting at the time, and he was able to see into the water from his higher angle.

Nothing had been said between us for quite some time when suddenly, he screamed like a girl and fell backwards over the rear seat, ending up with his butt on the bottom of the boat, his back against the outboard motor, and his feet up in the air. I turned to look at him, and his face was as white as a sheet. I didn't say anything; I just looked at him questioningly.

He sat there in a daze for a moment and then said, "It was an alligator, a God damn alligator."

I started to laugh and just said, "What?"

He had been casting a bucktailed, single-bladed spinner that was about ten inches long. A muskie had followed it into the boat, with the bucktail section in its mouth. The fish, according to Gene, was six feet long, nearly as long as the boat we were riding in, and it scared the crap out of him. I don't know how long I laughed at him, but we got a good chuckle. We reminisced about this for years. Sadly, my friend passed away a few years ago.

We made another trip to west central Minnesota in mid-October. The colors were wonderful; fall fishing is supposed to be really good, but we planned it a little late. It was really cold and windy. We were trolling for walleye, and my hands were really cold. I had a hit, a really good one, but my hands were so cold that I couldn't grip the rod; it just flew out of my hands and out of the boat. Lee was able to snag it and retrieve it, but he wouldn't let me live that down, either. I guess that made us even.

Alright, I'll get back to the sales dinner now. It's really worth waiting for.

We went off to dinner at Port Edward's with our wives. This was a very nice thing to do for the Sales Department. Port Edward's is a rather expensive place, and it was not going to be a cheap evening for the company. But let me add here the owner once told me he didn't care who I entertained for business, but he wanted to make sure I put on a real dog and pony show. He said he wanted our customer to remember it. This is good advice to anyone in sales.

Anyway, we were all having a good time. Gene, being a friend, knew I had accepted another position and was going to turn in my resignation. But to my surprise, he also knew something else that I didn't know. He couldn't wait to see my reaction, so he and his wife sat across the table from Jan and me. Jane was sitting next to me, with her husband on the other side.

During the dinner, our owner stood up and made a speech. He talked about what a good job everyone had done and how we had contributed to a very good year. He said he was proud to be able to recognize and award a plaque to the salesman of the year ... me.

I heard the nice applause but was in total shock. I turned to Gene and just stared at him. Inwardly, I wanted to kill him. He started to laugh so hard and long that he actually fell out of his chair.

Jane turned to me and said, "Steven, this is the first time I have ever seen you speechless."

I told her that she didn't know the half of it.

I turned in my notice a week later. It was not a pretty scene.

I digress, offering up a flashback. Here is a little more background that might be fun.

It's a toss-up as to whether family-owned businesses are weirder than others. I've worked for both, and they can both seem very strange in their own ways. Years ago, when I was a very young lad just out of high school, I worked for the largest company in my hometown. This was my first real job, and it was a family-owned company. It didn't hurt that my father had been in the Purchasing Department there for over thirty years. It was one of the leaders in forced heating systems. My father had gotten a job there just before World War II broke out. He returned to work there after he got back from the Pacific campaign in 1946. He had been stationed in Manila, the Philippines, as part of the occupation forces and worked at returning land to the proper owners, who had been displaced by the Japanese. Dad always said this company made the finest heating systems in the business. There was real pride in the workmanship then, but when labor unions got involved and started quota systems in the factory, quality went down the toilet; he often said it was a miracle that anything went out the back that even ran. My father once told me this cute story:

Every summer, the plant shut down for a two-week vacation. There was always a skeleton crew doing various jobs. Dad and the other executives took one week of their vacation then, and the other week some other time. During this shutdown period, there were always jobs going on that would normally have disrupted production. These executives were always assigned to oversee these projects. Dad had been assigned to oversee the paving of a ramp leading onto one of the loading docks. He tried to stay away as much as possible, so as not to upset the foreman, whose job it was to get the job done. But when he stopped by to see how the project was coming along, he noticed that one of the common laborers was none other than the owner's son. Now let me describe him. He was about five foot nine and weighed about 135 pounds. This was late June, it was about 100 degrees, and here was the owner's son, wrestling with hundred-pound bags of cement.

This whole picture seemed strange to Dad. My father approached him, pulled him aside, and asked him, "Ah, tell me, what the heck are you doing? You are the owner's son. What's going on?"

He responded, "Look, my dad called me a lazy, no-good bum. I told him that he could give me any damn job in the plant, and I could do it. Here I am."

The company occupied six city blocks; one building had a laboratory where new products were designed, built, and tested. This was where my brother worked as a draftsman while he was in high school and college. I worked there my first summer after high school as well. I'm not sure what I was, just a common helper, I suppose. I was told to do whatever anyone wanted me to do. I was not going to turn eighteen until August that summer, and the insurance didn't cover anyone under eighteen, so I was not allowed to even touch anything electrical. I was assigned to work under a man who ran the tool crib. He would check out tools and motors and small parts; it operated much like a library. He was a very talented machinist in his own right and had a very nice lathe in the crib. The only reason he was isolated here was that he was such a premier asshole that he couldn't work with anyone else, and no one could stand to work with him. So rather than fire a talented toolmaker, they gave him his own machine and isolated him from everyone else. I had to work with him. Wow, what a challenge. He treated me terribly.

I am not a prude, and as a college freshman, I was fairly world-wise, but I had never met anyone as crude, vulgar, boorish, and rude as him; he was a general pig. He kept a photo of two horses mating and showed it around like it was a girlie picture. Each morning, there was a coffee wagon that toured around the company and sold coffee, milk, and sweet rolls. One morning, I was standing in line, and the gentleman in front of me started up a conversation; it continued as we sat together until the break was over. When I returned to the tool crib, the toolmaker asked me if I was bucking for a better job. I told him I had no idea what he was talking about. It seems that the guy I spent fifteen minutes drinking coffee with was none other than the son of the owner. We didn't bother introducing ourselves, and I had no idea who he was. He was just being friendly.

The tool crib was a chain-link cage that had dark green shelving separated into small bins on three walls. Behind the crib was a very narrow aisle. Periodically, men would walk back there and stick a squirt gun barrel through one of the holes and squirt him when his back was turned. It drove him nuts. When he went on the two-week summer shutdown, I had control of the tool crib. I cleaned it up and ordered everything that everyone needed from local suppliers (he acted as a purchasing agent for the laboratory). One day that week, while I was away from the crib, some of the boys strung a copper tube from the aisle behind the crib to over the desk where I sat. They attached a funnel to one end and poured water into funnel so that I got drenched. I found out who did it, and we agreed that I hadn't seen a thing. I agreed not to take it down on the condition that I could be present when they baptized my boss. I don't think I've ever seen anyone quite that angry. It was great. I acted completely surprised, of course.

One of the little jobs they gave me was to sweep the floors. The laboratory floors were polished, and they showed every speck of dust. I was asked to fill in for the janitor, who was a graduate of the local mental institution. I am not kidding. He really was. He always seemed to be a nice guy, but I was told he had a slight temper problem. He could become violent without any warning. You know the saying that you have to "walk on eggshells" with someone, well, in this case, it was really true. But people would throw things at him, such as little rolled-up balls of putty, just to see if they could get him upset. The old saying that the only difference between men and boys is the price of their toys. Men can be so immature at times.

I got "stolen" from the crib (that's how my boss described it) by one of the engineers. He was a really good guy. He was in the process of inventing a furnace that ignited by an automobile spark plug. This would eliminate the need for a pilot light, and it would last almost forever because it only needed to fire long enough to start the gas burning. The heat exchanger that he was designing was made up of dozens of tubes that needed to be welded into place. My real job was to assist the welder. As time went by the welder taught me to arc weld. It was a lot of fun and very educational. The most fun was that the area I worked in was directly in front of the tool crib. My previous boss was there and watched me working for someone else. He was mad all the time anyway, so my working there only added to his frustration.

Keep in mind that I was not eighteen yet, and I was not covered by their insurance. Therefore, I would not be covered in case of an accident. I was strictly forbidden from touching anything electrical. So there I was, with a huge heat exchanger between my legs, welding tubing into this heat exchanger. Little did I know that the VP of the laboratory was standing behind me. When I lifted the welding mask, I saw him. I figured my days at the lab were over. He bent over to observe my work, said, "Good job," patted me on my shoulder, and walked away. I guess he figured I was being watched carefully, which I was.

The next summer, I got a really good-paying job at a junkyard. Yes, another family-owned business. The owner wouldn't be happy that I called it a junkyard, but that is what it was. He would buy scrap metal from anyone and everyone, clean it up (by that I mean make sure that the base metal of each object was not corrupted with another), and sell it to companies that melted it down for recycling. It was a very lucrative business. I was well paid and also learned some metallurgy, which turned out to be of real value to me years later when I got into the fastener business. It was the most physically demanding job I've ever had. I used to dump, by hand, fifty-gallon drums full of scrap metal; they weighed up to three hundred pounds each. They had been kept inside of railroad box cars that had been sitting sealed up outside in 100 degree temperatures. The temperature inside these cars was over 130. But it was good money.

The next two summers, I was away at college. I worked summers for the largest highline construction company in the United States. The home office was in my hometown, and I was fortunate to get this job. It paid very well, which came in handy since I was also a newlywed. This was not a family-owned company. But again, I worked with a very strange group of men. These were linemen. You know the song "Wichita Lineman" by Glen Campbell? Well, these guys are a very strange breed of cat. They go to jobs all over the country, live out of cheap motels for five days a week, and then try to get to their homes over the weekends. They drink every night and are forever living with real danger. I was classified as a groundman/truck driver. I was a gofer. I did all the heavy work. The first summer I worked for them, the foreman I worked under was not a nice guy. He was nasty to everyone, but especially me. I was a college boy. That first summer, because of his ineptness, a man got burned on a 13,800-volt line. I was there when it happened, and it was the most horrible thing I had ever seen. The most amazing thing was that he survived. But it happened directly as a result of our foreman's stupidity.

The second summer, I worked on another crew that was building a line across country. Thankfully, the foreman was much better, and no one got hurt. But these experiences really opened my eyes to another side of life that I was protected from by my middle class, Presbyterian family.

I drove an asphalt truck one summer while I was teaching, and I worked for six months for one of the major meat-packing companies. Again, this was not a family-owned company, but you meet a strange breed of cat when they slaughter and cut up six thousand hogs a day. I thought that many of these guys were pretty crude, but maybe this had something to do with the fact they worked in an abattoir.

During my formal study of history and the topic of unions, I learned that there was a time when employees had to do something to provide better working conditions, better pay, and benefits that made a better life for them and, as it turned out, a more profitable company. Unions can, sometimes, grow to be their worst enemies.

The meat-cutters union made some unreasonable demands on the company. The company finally warned the union to back off some of their demands, or else. You might wonder what else they could do. How about selling the plant to a competitor and letting them deal with these issues? The local union called their bluff, and guess what? They sold the plant to a competitor, and nearly all the jobs went away.

The really sad story here is that people in this little town pooled their money and invested $1 million to build the plant. It was a wonderful financial boost for a community that was badly in need of something to improve their standard of living. They did raise the money, and it worked wonders.

After the plant was sold, almost no one local was employed there. The new owner bussed workers in from a nearby urban area. This was totally foolish and never should have happened.

When I think back on the jobs I've done to make a little money, it has been a weird journey. I have baled hay, which nearly killed me, since I have asthma. I sacked at Osco Drug (for $0.25/hour, no kidding). I taught swimming classes and manned a cage at the local YMCA for nearly no pay at all. I unloaded oak lumber from a railroad car for a furniture manufacturer. I did menial tasks at a furnace factory. I worked at a junkyard, where I learned a little about metallurgy. I was a ground man truck driver for a highline company. I drove a truck for an asphalt company. I taught school and coached for three years. Finally, I sold screws. I have worked for and dealt with all types of people, ranging from some really low-class guys to what you might call the upper class. All these experiences taught me some degree of tolerance; I learned how to listen to and read people, which is a good basis for sales.

I taught school and coached sports for both boys and girls at a small Catholic school. The pay was terrible, but I had the time of my life. Financially, I had to make a decision. In the 1970s, schoolteachers were a dime a dozen. I was considering attending a management class at the meat-packing company. Thank goodness that didn't happen, since they later sold out. The placement office at my college offered me a chance to apply for a teaching/coaching position in the Chicago area.

CHAPTER 10

FIVE YEARS OF PRISON WITH ANOTHER FAMILY-OWNED BUSINESS

Time to get back to my fastener journey.

I didn't know it when I started, but there was an in-group and an out-group at what I'll call Apex Fasteners. The owner's eldest son was the head of the in-group, and the president, who the owner had hired to run his company, was the head of the out-group. I was given the title of the assistant to the vice president. This put me in the camp of the enemy right off the bat. They didn't want me to start for a while, so I had to bide my time before giving Gemini the customary two-week notice. (Traditionally, when a salesperson in the fastener industry gives a two-week notice, they are asked to clean out their desks at once and leave immediately. Evidently, the management thinks that you are going to steal something. Of course, if you were going to do that, you would have done it long before giving your notice.)

I had ten years of experience selling distributors. I had almost no OEM contacts. The management at Apex had the philosophy that fastener distributors were their competition and did not want to help them by selling them anything. I felt this was going to be an issue. After three years, the man who was going to call me "the next day" finally did call me. Still, I felt that working directly for two real gentlemen who were extremely well respected in the business, I should be able to learn a lot from them.

I was intrigued by the prospect of working under these two men; one was the president, the other the VP of sales. Both men had been in the industry for many years and worked for some of the most prestigious companies, and both had been in positions of great influence with those companies. I hoped to learn from them. They were both past retirement age. That is how they both came to work together at Apex. I had heard about the past problems at Apex, but I was assured by these two men, along with a few others, that these problems had been taken care of. They were wrong. I did not know it at the time, but the owner's son had been forced to hire me to establish business with, what he considered, the enemy.

This reminded me of something I want to include in the book: descriptions of screws, nuts, and bolts. I promised you readers that I was not intending to make fastener experts out of you, but a little knowledge might be helpful and fun.

Every fastener company uses their own abbreviations on their paperwork and inventories. But there are a few that are more popular than others. Now, people who have been dealing with these products can usually figure out what another company's abbreviations stand for by a process of elimination. But for a rookie to try to do it can become really humorous. Like the girl who wanted to know what kind of wood they make wood screws out of. Oh, dear.

Then another time, I got a call from an OEM buyer who started the conversation this way: "Hi, I'm Al from Benson Co. I'm looking for a bolt."

So I said, "You've come to the right place; we sell lots of them. Do you know the size?"

His answer was no.

I asked him if he knew the material the part he was looking for was made of, what was the head style, how long is it, and so on. His answer to everything was no. So I asked him if he had a blueprint of this bolt. He said no, but he had one on his desk. So I asked him if he could send it to me.

He said, "Well, no, it's the only one I have."

Now in cases like this, I become a little less charitable. I told him I couldn't read minds. I asked him if he could take a picture of it and send that to me.

He said, "Yeah, I can do that."

Eventually, I did get the order.

It becomes interesting when a person leaves one industry and goes to another completely different one, and both of them use the same abbreviations for completely different things. My boss at my second company was married to a lovely girl whose father owned a wholesale fish business. Right out of college, he went to work at the fish market.

He was a real rookie and had a lot to learn about marketing, buying, and distributing fish around the Chicago area. One of the terms he learned was the shrimp are sold according to weight count. Like how many per pound. The fewer per pound, the larger the shrimp and thus higher the price. They also have a designation of P&D, which stands for peeled and deveined. Much later, after he had moved on the fastener business, he ran into the same abbreviation.

He sheepishly asked, "What the heck are peeled and deveined screws?"

In the fastener business, when you ask a supplier for a quote, it is referred to as a P&D. That stands for Price and Delivery

Alright, getting back to my days at Apex.

Everywhere I have ever worked, whether a school, a junkyard or a fastener factory, there was a certain amount of political infighting and backstabbing. I have always tried to stay clear of all that. It helps if you don't get too close to the people you work with on a personal level. These things are nonproductive and frankly a waste of time. But I had never seen anything like what went on here. The majority of the nitpicking, backstabbing, political infighting was not among the employees but between members of the family itself. They all seemed to resent and distrust each other. They were all intelligent and talented in their own way, but they can't stand one another.

Where this all started, I had no idea. But from the very first day, I was intentionally put into the enemy camp. As I said earlier, I was the assistant to the vice president, who was not family. He was under the president, who was not family, either. There was another very influential person there. He was an engineer who ran Sunshine Screw, one of their branches, and was loved by everyone from top to bottom.

I might add here that this is very rare. You seldom find a person this talented. He wanted me to move to Sunshine for a couple of reasons. The main one was that I was trying to get some nice distributor business, most of which was run at his company. If I had been allowed to do that and was left alone, I might have stayed with them longer.

I must digress a bit here and explain a little about the family. First, you have Senior, who started Apex in the late 1940s. He built the company from the ground up and was a really fine gentleman. He wanted to stay close but did not want the stress of day-to-day management. He decided to step back, and knowing there was infighting among his children, he decided to hire an old friend who was being put out to pasture to take over the reins. He, in turn, knowing how screwed up the Sales Department was, hired an old friend who had been VP of sales for a big company.

The eldest son was a bit scatterbrained. The younger son, well, I'll explain more about him. One of his two daughters wanted nothing to do with the company; the other daughter was unmarried and worked as the accountant. The three working children kept getting in each other's way.

The older son was a very nice guy, very bright. He was like a one-man think tank. His mind worked so fast that he stuttered. He had dozens of wonderful ideas. Unfortunately, though, he rarely followed through on them. Apex spent a lot of money on numerous ideas that were total busts. He was always on the outs with his younger brother and his sister.

Well, getting back to Sunshine Screw, the branch company. To give you some idea of how this family worked. My friend Rick was promoted to run this branch. The older son called Rick and proceeded to tell him he was excited that he was leading the branch. He was going to move his office over there as well, and he and Rick were going to take it over. They were going to ignore the home office and were really going to make things happen.

Rick had no idea what all this meant, but he went ahead and did his own thing. A few minutes after this call, he got a call from the younger son. He told Rick how happy he was that his brother was moving to Sunshine and told Rick to watch him very closely and let him know everything that his idiot brother was up to.

Now, my friend is no fool. This was panning out to be very tough balancing act. So he hopped in his car, drove back to the parent company, and met with their father. In the meeting, he related what the two sons had done and explained that they put him in a really tough position. The father sympathized with him and agree that this was not fair. He really wanted Rick to be vice president of Sunshine, and his duties would be spelled out as time went by. But for now, he was to let him know whatever his two idiot sons were up to. Poor Rick drove slowly back to his office, totally confused as to what to do now. This was proving to be a no-win situation.

This example really shows how counterproductive this sort of in-fighting can be.

When I started, there was only one person I knew who had worked there, and that was my friend Rick. He had gone his separate way before I was hired. There was a purchasing agent there when I started who I knew a little about. Her father was a man named Dan who owned a major import company. Why she didn't work for her father, I never knew and never found out. She was the only person I thought I could talk to and get the inside stuff everyone needs to know in an effort to get along. After I was there just a few days, I asked her about the old man who swept the floors and cooked food in the company kitchen. She laughed and told me it was none other than the owner of the company. He was basically retired and tried not to get involved in the everyday working of the company, but he couldn't stay away. He would come in every day and putter around, doing whatever he felt needed to be done.

She also told me not to feel bad for not knowing who he was; she said, "Heck, I thought he was the janitor for the first month I worked here."

To give you readers an idea of how strange this company was, I will give you a few examples. Aside from having a working kitchen, they also had an antique car room. There was a Model A Ford, and old Rolls-Royce, and a Continental convertible from the sixties. That's the one where the doors open opposite each other. There was an old motorcycle, but it wasn't an antique.

Most manufactures have tool cribs, where the tools needed to make these screws are inventoried, and normally, there is a tool-and-die man employed to rework this tooling. This saves time and cuts costs, and most companies do it. Here, the crib took up a very large area and employed four or five toolmakers. The factory manager had been one of the original partners. He had sold his share of the business many years before. He was Croatian and hired a number of Croatian buddies to work as toolmakers. These were all very talented men. There were so many of them that they were often asked to work on things that had nothing to do with fasteners.

Some companies focus on the processes that need to be done to sell fasteners. Heat treating, for example, is done to harden screws that either cut or form threads into harder material. Another is to apply plating over the raw steel parts. Some companies do both, and I was familiar with one of them. The owner of one of these companies called me once and asked me to have dinner with him. At this meeting, he asked if I was interested in helping him start a new manufacturing company. Wow, what a compliment. I asked him why he wanted to start a new business. He explained that he was working on a new process in plating that could revolutionize the industry. I thanked him for the compliment but said he should marry himself with a distributor that could apply this new process to everything and not just what he could manufacture.

He asked if I could recommend anyone. Yes, I could: my good friend at Regal. I happened to know that he was selling a company that made windows and doors. All the screws they used had to be in 410 stainless steel. It is much more expensive than carbon steel and slightly harder. But hardened carbon steel is harder yet. If his new process could be put over steel parts, making them harder and nearly ten times more corrosion resistant and at a much lower price, it could be a huge advantage. I was asked to put the two together. The three of us had another meeting, and it turned out to be very good for both companies. Nothing for me, personally, although this was a determining factor later when I was offered to go to work for Regal.

Another event happened with this heat treating/plating company. One of our major accounts had only one customer, one of the big three automotive companies. We were making screws that went into their new in-board computers. The finish spec was complicated and intended to reject solder. That usually worked really good, but sometimes not so good. The assembly went through what is called a wave solder bath. There were times when tiny little solder balls would cling to the heads of the screws. If these happened to break off inside a computer, it would really mess it up.

I actually went to the plant and witnessed this. I called our plater and asked him for help. He suggested his new process might work. I asked him why he felt that way, and he simply did not know. He didn't invent it to reject solder. It worked perfectly. In fact, so perfectly that our customer wanted to send in some of their management to visit our plater.

Here is where the fun began. We set up a meeting and plant visit. The plating company gave them what I've always called a fifty-cent tour. We reconvened back in the owner's office, where the questions began.

They wanted to know why it worked so well. "Don't know."

They wanted to know what was in the process. "Won't tell you."

They wanted to know why. "It is patent pending."

They said they were not interested in stealing it. "Good."

They wanted to know if it was safe. He said, "Yes, you can drink it if you would like; it won't hurt you."

They then very dramatically said. "Maybe you don't understand; we're, you know, ABC Automotive Co."

He said, "Oh, go f—-k yourself."

I tried not to laugh. They all left in a huff. It was really fun to see someone not cave in to one of the big three.

For instance, the company owners all belonged to a well-known country club. They considered themselves to be quite the golfers. Once or twice a year, they would host a lamb roast for the members; they'd invite some of their better customers and treat them to a day of golf and a barbecue. They cooked whole lambs, legs of lamb, and dozens of chickens. The chickens posed a problem. The tool crib boys designed and built a chicken cooker that could roast something like sixty-four chickens at the same time. They put the on a trailer and towed it to the golf course. It was a V-shaped frame over a central charcoal basin that had numerous rotating spits, all operating from one motor, and all were connected by a series of gears. It was a neat idea. But I guarantee that based on the time, tooling, and parts involved, this was the most expensive chicken cooker in the world.

This was only one of the many projects they were given over the years; besides the chicken cooker, they made dog houses and whatever else the owners assigned to them.

I had worked for a number of companies at this point and thought I had been treated fairly. There were always people I liked and a few I thought were not so nice. This company treated people very unfairly. The owners didn't like or trust their employees any more than they liked or trusted their own relatives. I had never worked for a company where so many people went out of their way to steal from them. I guess if you make really sharp people mad enough, they either leave or find a way to get back at the owners.

Before I went to work for them, an employee stole their secret process that made cylindrical bearings on a cold header. These bearings are put into housings. They are usually made by way of screw machining, which is a very expensive process. They had invented a secret way of making them on cold headers at a very high speed, with almost no scrap. They could save customers a lot of money while making a huge profit. An employee stole this process and started his own company.

They had a branch plant down South that made really exotic parts, some of which were made out of copper. If you know anything about the cost of metals, you know how expensive copper is. It was discovered that a few of the people at this factory were not just stealing the raw material but were actually making parts and selling them on the side (and, of course, selling the scrap copper).

Shortly after I left the company, it was discovered that one of their toolmakers had been stealing all the carbide scrap. The tools needed to make screws can be made out of either steel or carbide. The broken steel parts are worthless; carbide, on the other hand, is very valuable and can be recycled. How strange it was that they never had any scrap carbide. One of their loyal toolmakers was taking it and selling it on the side. He ended up with a better tool shop in his house than the one where he worked. I said earlier that some of these men were intelegant. He would have gotten away with it, except he started to advertise. Oops.

The VP of sales, my boss, was one of the finest people I ever worked for. He was a real gentleman and a true sales professional. He was possibly the kindest person I've ever known in this industry.

One day, the sister, the bookkeeper, went running through the office weeping; this is not something you see every day. I stuck my head into my boss' office and asked him what was going on.

He called me into his office, rolled his chair around next to me, put his arm around my shoulder, and said, "Steven, it seems that we have a little problem."

I was a bit concerned and asked him what had happened.

He said, "It seems that the auditors just left, and they discovered that the company made a million dollars more than they had figured on."

Keep in mind that I'm not the brightest; you know, I was raised out West and not up on how these things work, so I was a bit confused. To me, that should be a good thing.

So I asked, "And this is a bad thing?"

He replied, "Well, it is when you already paid out the rent checks."

It took me a moment to translate this. Then it came to me.

I said, "Uh oh, and she has already spent her share without paying the taxes?"

All he said was, "Yep."

Customers often complained about how their screws functioned. This was almost never due to the quality of the screw. More often, there were other reasons. One might be a bad design, but not the screw's design; rather, it's a mistake on the part of an engineer who is not a fastener expert. He thinks that he needs one type of screw that's not meant to be used the way he thinks it should.

Another reason, which is much more common, is misuse. I'll give you a prime example. We had been making some really long screws that are part of an assembly used in installing special roofing. Some of these are over thirty inches long. We had a customer complain that they were bent. This was absolutely impossible. You see, the screws were packed in tall boxes by dropping them through a tube so they stood up in the boxes. A bent one would not go through the tube. Get it? My boss, over retirement age, mind you, went to the job site and got up on the roof to watch how they installed them. Ready? They would start by taking a screw out and hitting it on the head with a hammer to get it started. Huh, I wonder who they got bent?

Another good example occurred with one of our major customers. They had only one customer, one of the big three automotive companies. They supplied us with automotive prints of their parts. There was a dimension on all their tapping screws and thread-cutting screws that was impossible to measure accurately. The reason was that it was on the angle point of the screw, and once the part is threaded, the dimension changed as you turned the screw. We sold them in many different sizes, and they would send us a letter of nonconformance each and every time. Our QC manager basically ignored them by responding with a form letter that said something like we are looking into it. Now, keep in mind that the parts function just fine. They were not rejecting anything.

It got to a point that something had to be done to clean up this mess. I went to the plant with our sales rep and our QC manager; we met with the head buyer, their QC people, and their incoming inspectors. They stated their feelings, and we explained that this measurement could not really be measured once the parts were threaded.

I finally suggested that we all go into their incoming inspection area and watch how they measured the parts, and we, as the supplier, would do it the same way.

Their head engineer said to me, "What if we are wrong?"

I said, "You can't be wrong. You're the customer."

He knew that the parts all went to their customer, who supplied the print, and said, "That's where you are wrong."

I thought for a moment and suggested they contact the customer's tech center and ask them to act as a referee. A few days later, I got a call from the head engineer. He said he had gotten a response; he was informed that it was only a reference dimension, and it didn't mean anything. Frankly, that is what we had been saying all along. But the customer is the customer.

Apex treated their employees badly, and that caused them a lot of problems. It was this sort of Scrooge attitude that caused the president to walk out. During the plant shutdown between Christmas and New Year's Day, he was going over the year-end figures and discovered that there had been plenty of money to give all the employees a nice Christmas bonus. No one, except the family, had gotten a dime. When we returned from the shutdown, his office was empty. No one knew why he was gone. He showed up at the diner where most of us had lunch and told us what had happened.

I've been told I have a problem with authority figures, but I don't think I do. I learned that respect is something earned; it can't be commanded. I have worked with many people I respect, and I always gave them my respect. Unfortunately, I've also worked for people who did not deserve mine or anyone else's. I've often found occasion to have some fun where there isn't any. Here's an example:

One day, I was walking through the office when I noticed an Orkin pest control guy. He was on his hands and knees in front of the sister's office, holding a small magnifier to the door casing. I asked him what was doing. He said he was trying to determine where the small flies were coming from that had invaded the office. I could have told him to go back into factory where there was a garbage can next to the lunchroom door; it seldom got emptied and was full of banana peels and so on. It was a breeding place for thousands of fruit flies. I didn't want to tell the man his job, so I just watched him for a while.

I told him they were not new; we had had them for a long time. The sister interrupted and said they were, in fact, new. So I decided to have a little fun with him. I told him they were crude oil flies. He asked me what they were.

I said, "They are a variety of fly in China that lays their eggs in the crude oil that is used to ship screws in to protect them from corrosion, and then after the screws get shipped to the United States, they hatch out into flies."

He said he wanted to see for himself. So I took him back into the warehouse where the import kegs were kept. Now, to get there, we had to walk right by the lunchroom, where these fruit flies were simply swarming.

Years ago, imported fasteners used to come in wooden kegs, but they now came in metal kegs. I walked him through the building, past the factory, and into the warehouse, down a ramp to where the imported material was stored. When I left him, he was up against a metal keg, examining it with his eyepiece. When I returned to the office, the son said he couldn't believe I had done that. I told him the flies he was looking for came from the lunchroom, and all that needed to be done was to clean out the trash bins more often, and that would take care of the flies.

Around twenty minutes later, the Orkin man came back into the office, paused, and said, "You know, I think you're right."

Everyone got a good laugh, except the Orkin man, who didn't get the joke, I guess.

One of my longtime distributor customers was in the New York area. What a neat place, a huge landscaped building. They did their own heat treating and plating in-house. There was an elevator between floors. It was very impressive. They had two owners. The two sons of one of the owners handled the day-to-day sales and purchasing. I nearly always dealt with the one who handled the purchasing. I had been there many times and had a wonderful relationship with both sons. As it turned out, the president of our company was lifelong friends with one of the partners. Our branch factory did all the manufacturing for their parts. This was a very nice account due to these relationships.

We invited them to come to Chicago for a visit. We gave them a tour, had a nice lunch, and arranged a fancy dinner at a golf club. (Keep in mind that selling to distributors was considered aiding and abetting the enemy.) They were also taken to our home office. While they were at our home office, the younger son of our owner snubbed them. Three days later, I got a phone call from the buyer.

He said he had treasured our relationship for years but "nobody snubs me like that. I'm going to pull all our business." That represented over $200m dollars.

Our president was furious. I was offended. How's that for cutting off your nose to spite you face?

If you remember, one of the distributors I introduced Gemini to was Regal Fasteners. They were now doing a great deal of direct as well as shared business. It had developed into a very good relationship. I had an occasion to help Regal with an issue. It was rather technical, so I won't get into it, but it got Regal a lot of orders. This actually happened twice. I did this because he was a good friend.

After I had been working at this awful place for five years, I got a call from the owner of Regal, who invited me out to dinner.

During the meal, he said to me, "Are you ready to get the hell out of that place?"

I had never worked for a distributor. I had sold to dozens, but I had no OEM experience.

He said that OEMs are much easier to sell because "they aren't as smart as us."

It still caused me some concern. I knew I would have to basically start all over, from square one. We discussed the terms for three months, and then he offered me a deal that was "good for both of us."

I was anxious for a change, so I took it. Regal Fasteners was the fourth company I worked for. Talk about a gamble; I was going to work for a company that had three employees and nearly the same number of customers. As it turned out, this one lasted for almost twenty years.

CHAPTER 11

REGAL

I am not, nor have I ever been, a gambler. My upbringing was conservative. I was taught that owning is better than renting, and a penny saved is, well, you know. It was out of my comfort zone to go to work for a very small company, only three employees and the owner. They were totally a distributor company, selling only to the OEM, and I had almost no OEM customers, certainly none I could count on to follow me. I would have to be the only salesman, the purchasing agent, and the inventory control clerk; sometimes, I had to unload trucks and pack screws. Thanks to my fastener education, I knew how to do all these things.

The financial arrangement was fine, but I was not going to be paid unless I was able to deliver. I had confidence in my abilities, but when you are selling to the distributor, you have a customer who already needs something. When you are trying to sell the OEM, they already have a supplier; you have to offer something they don't already get. Screws are the cheapest commodity they have to supply, and the job is usually given to the low person on the totem pole. Purchasing agents for the end user usually don't want to rock the boat.

When we were discussing my terms, I asked for a grace period while I got started. We agreed on a wage. He added the incidentals and totaled up my cost to the company and then divided it by twelve. I had to ship that much profit to work there. He would then pay me 5 percent of the gross profit over that amount. I was told I had three months to perform. He would review my performance after each quarter. Does this sound like a gamble? For the first time, I felt that I might get paid for my efforts. I was free to do whatever I wanted to do, as long as I made money. The time limits set on how fast to start paying for myself seemed very short and I was afraid might cause a problem.

Here is how it worked out: After my first quarter, I had a few small orders but had not shipped a dime. He gave me another quarter. At the end of the first six months, I had covered the first quarter. He was pleased that I was making some headway. At the end of the third quarter, I was even. Tada. At the end of the first year, he wrote me a check for a thousand dollars.

He was pleased, I was pleased; everybody was happy, right? Well, all fun things can get ugly. Here's what happened to my year-end assessments:

Year 1 ... $1,000 Bonus
Year 2 ... $5,000 Bonus
Year 3 ... $10,000 Bonus
Year 4 ... Oops, here is where the terms changed; are you surprised?

Being the type of guy that I am, I always kept these records. After eighteen years, he should have been paying me $250,000 per year based on the original terms. He didn't.

Getting back to when I started, I knew I needed some sales representation. I needed sharp ones who could get me in the door of potential good customers.

As I told you earlier, there are good sales reps who are worth their weight in gold, and then there are others who, well, aren't. My first one came from my previous employment. I'll call him Tom. He was from Ohio. His family had been in the business for over a hundred years. They had been supplying the automotive industry for years. He had become a sales rep and was needing lines. One of the agencies he knew in Michigan that now represented my previous employer recommended him. I called him and asked him if he would like to come to work for me. He had never worked for a distributor and wondered how he would make any money.

I knew something he didn't. I asked him if he knew that he wasn't being paid commission on some of the accounts in his territory. This really upset him, of course. I then suggested that he would make more money with me, anyway. I had my first rep.

My first trip to Ohio was very interesting. I landed at Hopkins Airport, and Tom picked me up in his pickup truck. Off we went into the country.

I was a bit confused; aren't there a whole bunch of companies right there in Cleveland? He said we were going to call on a company that was sixty miles away.

One of the first inquiries he got for us was with this same company. Upon following up on the quote, I was told that our pricing was high. I was a little confused as to why we would waste our time traveling that far away to visit a company we already knew did not like our prices, when there were dozens of sales calls we could make in the same time right there in Cleveland. He told me that the buyer was really pretty, and I should meet her. He was not wrong; she was very attractive. In our meeting, we discussed the fact that our prices were all high, but she was unwilling to tell us how high. The entire inquiry was for standard hex bolts that anyone can import. I thought for a moment and asked her if they used nuts on these bolts, and she said that of course they used nuts. I asked what type. She tried to describe them to me. What she was trying to describe were serrated flange nuts.

Regal Fasteners was first established on one very large customer that really liked our owner. He had what we might call an in with the purchasing agent. She thought the world of him. One of the main products that Regal had been selling them was … ready? You guys are quick: serrated flange nuts. Yes, and they were the same sizes used on the quote in question.

I said to her, "You know what? I think I can save you some money on them."

We were able to get started doing business with three sizes of serrated flange nuts.

This grew over the years to over a $3 million account and over four hundred parts. How that all developed is a story in itself.

Many companies use mostly women on their production lines. There are a couple of good reasons for this. One is that women tend to handle tedious jobs better than men. Their concentration is better, and they make fewer mistakes. There is another reason (mind you, not a good one): Unfortunately, they work cheaper than men. The downside of this is that women are women. I don't mean to sound sexist, but they really can become complainers.

It is very helpful to have factory people on your side when you are supplying the OEM. Thanks to the efforts of my good rep, we had quite of few that were definitely on our side. I ounce got a call from the QC manager. He told me he had an issue with one of parts we were supplying. The annual volume on this part was around twelve million parts. It was used in five different locations in the factory. They had multiple girls at each production station installing these parts.

One of the women on one line complained that she got slivers in her fingers from these screws. The screw she was installing is called a Hilo. It has a helix thread with alternating high and low threads. It is intended to be used in plastic, and the high thread is very sharp. The theory is that they displace less material upon installation, which causes less fracturing of the boss, or mating part, it is going into.

Now it is possible for this to happen, but unlikely. As I explained, this screw alternates high threads and low threads. The high thread is very sharp. Small pieces of steel can peel off in the thread-rolling process. But these parts get tumbled in the manufacturing process, tumbled in cleaning, tumbled in heat treating, tumbled in plating, and tumbled yet again in packaging. The odds of her getting stuck by a splinter would be rare but not impossible. How serious was this? She was threatening to sue the company. The QC manager could not afford to ignore the issue. He told me we had to address this problem. I promised to research this thoroughly for him. I took two boxes of parts. There were 7m per box.

We went through every single part but were not able to find a single sliver. The QC manager told me that in the meantime, he took it a step further. He put a box of screws in a parts tumbler (this looks like a small cement mixer). He said that this seemed to take care of her problem. She was happy that he had done this for her, and she didn't experience any more problems.

On my next plant visit, the QC manager said he wanted me to meet our lady complainer. I told him I really didn't want to, but he said he wanted me to see what he had to put up with.

Upon being introduced she said, "Oh, you're the guy." She then told me her long sad story and said the QC manager was now taking all of her boxes and tumbling them especially for her; they were marked with a blue sticker. I confirmed that she was satisfied. She said she was much happier.

As we walked away from her, the QC manager asked me if I knew how they tumbled her parts.

I said sarcastically, "Let me guess: You merely put a blue sticker on them?"

He said, "Yep."

I told him he didn't need any psychologists there; he was becoming one himself.

While we were there, another worker complained that the screws she was installing were hard to drive. Another one doing the same job with the same parts ten feet away said she had no problem at all; the problem was the other lady was an "idiot." The frustrating thing is, these things had to be addressed, and the poor fastener supplier had to come up with a solution where there wasn't one. There was nothing wrong with the parts, but we were accused of causing the problem. It is a fact that fastener failures are caused by misuse and bad applications rather than bad parts. In the forty-plus years I have been in this business, I have seen only a few actual fastener failures due to the structure of the screw.

The PA that gave us our first orders retired. Her replacement was a truly professional purchaser. Diane was a wonderful buyer and was a good friend, which has everything to do with Regal being a good supplier. She was responsible for moving most of their fastener requirements to us.

I think the reader has already figured out that I was not your typical salesman. Neither was my sales rep. Every time we called on these folks, there were people we made it a point to contact. Many people in the factories, QC people, engineers, and support people. We always made it a point to ask if their top management people needed to speak to us for any reason. John, the general manager was not a very happy fellow. We were told that salespeople actually avoided him. We made a point of just saying hello, if nothing else.

It was near Christmas, and despite their rule that they could not accept any gifts, we would always get some nice things that could be shared by the entire Purchasing Department. It's sort of hard to refuse that. Our buyer was very pregnant, and my rep and I were informed that she had gone into labor. We were expecting her to be home with the newborn, so we decided to get her and her family a nice ham. I added a box of diapers. We had her address, so we drove to her house, not knowing if she would even be there. We drove up to her house, and the garage door was open with a car in it. Guess what? She had arrived from the hospital minutes before, with her new little girl. In comes these two stupid salesmen, bearing gifts. We were welcomed and even got to hold the baby. We didn't stay long and headed to the company with cookies and candy for the whole department. When we arrived at the office, the greeting we got was very surprising. They already learned that we had been to their boss's home and got to hold the new baby. They were all very jealous.

She was promoted to the director of purchasing, which meant we would be getting a new buyer. This concerned me, but she promised that the new person would be trained "properly."

As I said, we ended supplying over four hundred parts to them, many of which were not screws and to include them under the category of fasteners would be a stretch. I didn't know what they were, how they were used, and most importantly, where to get them. Remember the product shows that were in Columbus, Ohio? For once, I had a reason to be there. I needed to find a source for some of these things. I was turning from one aisle to another and ran into someone I had known for years. The booth she was representing had, years before, been an old distributor customer of mine. She was now the general manager. She and I were exactly the same age and had families at the same time. We always had things to talk about.

I asked her about herself and her company. I was told they were selling all kinds of proprietary parts. These were usually parts the dealer is required to have a license to sell. It also ended up that they had been selling parts to the larger corporation that owned my customer. From then on, as these new parts were turned over to us, I'd just call her, and she would either sell them to me or tell me where I could get them. It's good to be nice to people and make as many friends as you can. You never know.

As I said earlier, this wonderful lady who gave us most of their fastener business was very good at her job. This was recognized by management, and she was promoted to director of purchasing. She had to replace herself. This caused me a considerable amount of distress. She promised me she would "train this person properly." Her replacement was a delightful woman, a newlywed fresh out of college.

Regal was given dozens of parts that were not screws and nuts. I had no idea what some of them were or how they were used, but most importantly, I didn't know where to get them or how to price them. So when I finally was able to source them, I just asked my customer what they had been paying. Now, this is just not done. As you know by now, I'm not very traditional. She would tell me what she had been paying, and I was alarmed; they had been getting charged way too much. I would give them a legitimate price. This went on over a long period of time. We now had a new buyer. The first time this happened, I asked her what they had been paying, but she refused to tell me. I just told her to ask her boss.

She came back, said, "She said I'm supposed to tell you," and she did.

When I gave a much better price, she was shocked. She wanted to know if we were doing alright. I told her yes, but they had been paying way too much.

Another time, I had to raise a price on a part. She began to argue.

Being the smooth salesman I am, I told her, "Get over it. It doesn't mean anything to you. These parts are cheaper than the paper clips on your desk."

She wanted to check something out. When she called me back, she had actually checked out what I had said. She added, "You're right; they are cheaper than the paper clips. I'll change the price."

Everything continued on very smoothly. That is until her boss, my buddy, got a better job. Then her wonderful replacement got a better job. They had an assistant, who always filled in for them very admirably; she was overlooked for the promotion because she didn't have a college degree, which was really dumb. She could, and did, do the job wonderfully whenever she was needed. They hired a new buyer who proved to be a problem.

At the same time, they needed a new director of purchasing. Both proved to be a problem for us. Regal continued to do a good job for them until the end, which came as a combination of things, one of which was that my customer was close to going out of business.

There was one little event that proved a point for me about the cost of fasteners to the OEM. As I said much earlier, fasteners are considered a C item, which is a commodity item that just has to be available at all times. If that C item is not available and shuts the production lines down, it now becomes an A item. My rep and I were attending a two-day vendor meeting at Firestone Country Club. During the meeting, the new purchasing director, the one who was, shall we say, not so good, began throwing out numbers. Numbers that he probably should not have been advertising. We began writing them down. It proved one of my points that I had always believed. The four hundred parts we had been supplying represented less than 2 percent of the cost of their product. I had been working in a really down and dirty industry.

The buyer, who's responsible for purchasing fasteners, thinks it's a big deal. It isn't. The important thing is the service and not the cost. John, the general manager of this company wasn't friendly, but my rep and I would ask to see him every time we were in the plant, just to say hello. He once told us that Regal was not just the best fastener supplier they had; we were the best supplier of anything they ever had. How's that for a compliment?

I mentioned the last purchasing agent we had to work with, and she was a problem. This is a very indelicate story I will try to tell it as delicately as I can. Lori was an attractive young lady but there was something about her that bothered me. I think the reader knows now that good sales people learn to read the person they are trying to sell. I was told that she had alopecia and she wore a wig due to the problem. Later I leaned that is was not the case. She actually pulled her hair out. Her assistant called me once to tell me she was cutting the hair on her arms with a pair of scissors. During the last meeting we had with her she seemed very nervous. She actually pulled, what I'll call a "Sharon Stone" on my rep. If you don't know what I mean go watch the movie "Baic Instinct." My rep turned and look at me and had the expression of a deer in headlights. I do admit that I teased him about it, and still do.

All good things come to an end. They were made to believe that importing their fasteners direct from overseas was the way to go. It would be much cheaper. I tried to explain to them how wrong that idea was. The business they were in was making garage door openers, not fasteners. All of the liability is in the hands of the distributor. Imports are brought in all at once and paid for all at once. If there is a quality issue, they have to deal with it intenatioaly. The distributor warehouses the parts, and the OEM only pays for the parts they pull in for their use. Keep in mind, we shipped them a full semi-truck load every Tuesday and full straight-truck load on Thursdays. We had a large warehouse, just for fasteners. It just did not make sense when fasteners represented such a small percentage of their product's cost.

As it turned out, they were on their way out, anyway.

We had a final chance to quote the annual contract. The quantities were not correct on the quote. They were listed using the previous year's usages. The RFQ (Request For Quote) did not allow for the parts they would be buying direct from overseas. There was a large company that had been the main supplier to the parent company for years. We knew they would be quoting the package as well. They did nearly $6 million with the parent company; we did $3 million with the subsidiary. They had always wanted our portion.

Here's where it gets interesting. In years past, when I was in distributor sales I had sold them parts. I knew Donny, the GM, very well. We had not spoken in years, of course. We knew the quantities on the RFQ were wrong, but they did not. They, of course, won the contract and simply absorbed Regal. I waited what I thought was an appropriate length of time to make my call. I called my old customer to congratulate him on adding to their business. The conversation went something like this:

Me. "Hi, Donny, how are you doing? It's been a long time." He returned the pleasantry. I continued, "Congratulations on getting the contract."

His response was, "You SOB. We were excited about it and started buying parts overseas. Then we started to see the releases. We called them at once and wanted to know why the quantities were so small. They told me they didn't tell us to BUY anything."

I told him the whole story and said we knew what they were going to be doing with the bigger users, but I legally could not tell them.

The company that Regal was based on from the beginning went out of business, and these two represented nearly all of Regal's sales. I was getting close to retirement, but not quite. Where do I go from here?

All salespeople work in different ways. Many are successful in their own ways. I have always said that women have a huge advantage over men who are in sales. Why? I heard you ask. Here is my reasoning: If a woman knows the product and is fairly attractive (she doesn't have to be beautiful), and she calls on a male purchasing agent, all things being equal, guess who is going to get the business? Usually, a man wouldn't stand a chance. On the other hand, and I've seen this personally, if the saleswoman doesn't know the product, she will not be very successful. When I was at Gemini, the owner once told me that sales are made and continued through personalities; the price of fasteners is not that important. In many cases, he was correct. I have worked with many salespeople and rep agencies over the years, some of them women. Everyone works in their own way, and if they are successful and have a good relationship with the customers, who am I to question their methods?

The owner of Regal, my boss for nearly twenty years, once told me what he did to get business. He had been calling on this potential customer for a long, long time. He was told that his prices were competitive, close, but to keep trying. Finally, he got so frustrated and he started yelling at the buyer. He stood up on the guy's desk and began yelling to give him an order. The buyer begged him to get down; he gave him an order. You never know what might work.

I never went that far, but I have tried to shame a buyer into giving my company an order. I once told a buyer that she was not helping her company if she did not choose us as a supplier. I did not know at the time that her boss was listening in on our conversation. He called me the next day and gave us a five-thousand-dollar order. You just never know.

CHAPTER 12

ONE LAST DANCE

One of my vendors at Regal Fasteners was a small manufacturer in Rockford, Illinois. Their sales manager had become a good friend. He was close to retiring and suggested that I apply to them. He was constantly being pressured to stay in the office and work up pricing, and when he did, he was pressured to get out on the road and drum up business. He was a good friend and thought that since he lived in Rockford, he would stay there and work from the inside, and since I had good contacts, I could work from the outside, making local calls with my new reps, making road trips where necessary. I agreed to make weekly trips to the office.

A meeting was set up with the owner. I had never seen the place, and frankly, I was not very impressed. I told them I was not going to be driving to Rockford every day. At this late stage of my career in fasteners, I felt that I could make some of my own terms. I told them that with a computer connection to their office and a dedicated phone, I could start bringing them business they never had. I was offered the job with incentives (which they were never fulfilled). But unknown to me, they let my friend go at the same time. That should have been a sign for me. But I needed the job, so I accepted it.

Again, I made the bad choice of going to work for another family-owned business. At first, they were cooperative. I got the computer connection, the phone and car expenses, and so on. I wanted authority. I requested full authority of hiring and firing reps and salespeople. The owner agreed that was my job.

I began reviewing their sales and territories. The man who was fired in my replacement was kind enough to go over this, without the knowledge of the owner. I began by reviewing the territories, customers, and sales records, basically assessing the performance of the reps. It was clear to me that they had one or two reps who actually did something for the company. They had one who had some business but never left his house. Two or three did nothing. One had been dead for over a year. I went over this with the owner and made recommendations as to who to keep, who to replace, and who to try to convince to get to work and start again to perform or they would be gone. Reps can often establish a certain amount of sales and a limited number of accounts and then rest on their laurels.

I did what had to be done. My future as well as the company's depended on sales. I felt that some hard decisions had to be made, and with the approval of the top management, I made some changes. The one that bothered me the least was their oldest rep, who showed me absolutely no respect and refused to do anything I asked of him. He was gone.

The last two years I worked there, they had record sales. I know I was not the only reason for this success, but I do feel I was instrumental in it.

Here is where the problem came. My predecessor was being pulled and pushed. They wanted him to stay in the office and work up quotes and, in the next breath, to get out of the office and generate more sales. He was hoping that we would be there together as a team. They began to do the same to me. I was generating a lot of new business. Requests for quotes were coming in at a rather fast rate. I was being asked to come to Rockford every day to work up pricing on these quotes. I reminded them that as part of our original agreement, I was not going to drive to Rockford every day to do clerical work.

The owner's son was the guy who had to price them. He did not like working very hard. He especially disliked working up quotes. He had a buddy who lived in Rockford who had no experience, and they could pay him much less than me. But, most importantly, as I was actually told, I was old. They let go. I was not quite at retirement age. Could I have sued? Probably. Would it have been worth it? Not to me. These final few years were really not much fun, anyway.

I might give you readers an example of how unsophisticated this industry is. Intelligence and talent are not necessarily needed to own or manage a fastener company.

This last place I worked for had one big customer. The company was established on this account and had existed on it for ten years. They had agreed to a ten-year contract. Let me repeat that: ten years. With this contract coming to an end guess what the customer was demanding: price reductions. Just so we all agree, whenever contracts are coming to a close, customers often ask for price reductions, knowing this is totally out of the question, but it's always worth a try. I was being pressured to solve this problem since I was the sale manager, after all.

Logically, costs had increased over ten years, not decreased. One way to possibly show a savings would be to import some of their biggest users. They did not outsource anything. I went to two of my favorite importers I had used in the past, hoping to solve this issue. I gave them four parts to quote, based on one-third of the annual volume. These quantities were in the millions of parts. Now, read this carefully: The imported costs were higher than the domestic selling prices to their customer.

There was a big meeting with me, the rep, and all the management. I informed them of this problem and said they were in a tough position. I asked for the actual manufacturing cost on these parts. They didn't know and didn't know how to calculate them. They needed someone to do an actual time study to find out the real cost of the parts they made. I had learned to do this years ago and volunteered to do it for them, but just one element was missing, a very important one, one I could not come up with myself, and that was the overhead figure. I can do cost-plus, using labor rates and all the other factors that go into true costs, but without the real overhead rates, I couldn't do it. They didn't like what I told them. I guess some people can't handle the truth. My apologies to Jack Nicholson. To make themselves feel better, they blamed it all on me.

Training of employees, or should I say the lack of it, is something I've always been concerned with. Starting where I did was a huge advantage. I was given a real education. I was trained in all aspects of the fastener business. Far too often, companies put people on the phones who know nothing about the business. Purchasing people today look at a part number on a computer, match it with the current supplier, and place the order online. No one talks to anyone; no one knows what they are buying. They don't know what it looks like, how it's made, or how it works (or if it works). There are salespeople who don't know what they are selling. If they are calling on a customer with a problem, they don't know how it can be solved.

Some of this knowledge is needed to answer phones, and all of it is necessary to call on customers. Representatives may not be experts, but a person from the plant who visits a customer has to be able to answer questions and not appear to be a fool. I always went out of my way to make a pest of myself because I wanted to know functions. I was blessed to have salespeople working for me who knew how to really help a customer as well as sell a customer.

After forty years in the screw and bolt business, I had earned my PhD, at least that's what my friend from Rockford said of me. I became pretty darn good at what I did. I made money for every company I worked for. I always supported the company and did my best for them. This was a lesson I learned from my father, who told me, "Whatever you do for a living, do the best job you can; you end up spending a third of your life doing it, so make sure you enjoy it. If you don't enjoy it, do something else; life is too short."

I worked for a lot of companies that had a reputation for having, shall we say, difficulty with management. But I also have a reputation for being fair, civil, and respectful of everyone. I was paid a compliment from a previous employer that did not come directly from him. It actually came from two different people. It was paid to me by one of those difficult managers. I heard he said one of the biggest mistakes he ever made in business was allowing me to leave and go to another company.

As I wrote earlier in this book, my mother once said I would either be a teacher or a salesman. She was right on both counts. I was a teacher and a coach, and a pretty good one. And for over forty years, I was a salesman, and I'm proud to say, a pretty good one. I have no regrets.

CHAPTER 13

ONE MORE JOB

I was a bit short of complete retirement and a year or so too young. I did not want to work in the fastener business anymore. I was tired of working for people I did not respect and who did not know as much as me about the industry. I also knew I was not willing to sell my services cheap, and that's what employers in the fastener business try to hire.

Working full time did not sound like fun. I did some checking around, and a very good friend of mine worked for a local golf course. The pay was terrible, but you got free range balls, free golf, and a discount on food and merchandise. It was part time, so the demand on my time was minimal.

The guys who were starters and rangers were really nice. The types of people we had to deal with ranged from very low handicap golfers who knew the rules of golf down to hackers who have no idea of the basic ground rules, either of the course or of the game itself. Our job was to nicely and politely teach the general public how to follow these rules, not get hurt or hurt other players, and not tear up the golf course.

So I applied for the job and was hired, and for the next five years, I worked as combination starter and gapper. You might wonder what the heck a gapper is. It is a ranger, who drives around the course and makes sure the golfers are obeying all the rules and keeping pace. Following the rules is pretty easy really. If there is any question, they are printed on the back of the score cards. Keeping pace, again, is logical. Each group is expected to keep up with the group ahead of them, but not too close.

That sounds like pretty easy duty, doesn't it? Well, yes, it is, most of the time. There were times when those customers don't play by the rules, don't keep pace, and can, at times, become unruly.

I had some comical experiences over the five years I worked there. At the time, they didn't seem very funny, but after thinking about them and discussing them with the other rangers, they usually became very funny. Here are a few of those situations.

One of our local golf courses is very much a public course. It is a park district course. It is not supported by local taxes; it is solely self-sufficient. It is a golf course; people play golf there. They hit a small, very hard projectile that can kill you if you get in the way. This little white ball is struck by a funny crooked stick that if it hits you in the head, you are dead. Considering this, it is not a public park. This proved to be a point of controversy any number of times. Actually, the very first day I worked there, I was driving down the first fairway and got a call on my walkie-talkie. I was informed that a lady was jogging on the second hole.

I caught up with her and asked her what she thought she was doing. She said she was going for a run. I nicely told her that this was a golf course and she couldn't jog here. She said she was from Ohio and didn't know she couldn't run there.

I, again trying to be nice, asked her if there were golf courses in Ohio. Golf balls are really hard, and getting hit by one would hurt. I nicely directed her back to a road. After all, if she got hit by a car, it wouldn't be the responsibility of the course.

Another time, I saw a man taking a stroll with his wife, child, and their dog. I told him he couldn't do that; this was private property, and, well, again, it is a golf course. He advised me that he was a local taxpayer, and since his taxes supported this course, he had every right to walk there. When I corrected him, telling than no tax money is dedicated to the golf course, he asked for my name. I was happy to give it to him. I suggested that he call my superior and gave him his name. I then asked for his name in return. He didn't offer it. I told him that he would still have to vacate the property.

One of the logical spots for a ranger to sit is between holes number three and four. You have a good view of quite a bit of the front nine; the third hole is a long par three, and four, which parallels it going the other way, is a par five that has a water hazard at about two hundred yards. It can become a bottleneck. On one of the first days I worked, it had been raining, and the rule of the day was cart path only. If you don't play golf, that means the golf carts must stay on the paved paths. They are not allowed on the fairways. Wih all the rain making the fairways soft, golf carts can really tear them up. Having a good view of the second hole, a golfer sliced his drive off number two, across the eighth hole, and into the rough on the other side of eight. I watched him drive his cart across two and then across eight, and then hit his ball back onto number two. By the time he got back to the cart path on two, I was sitting there waiting for him. I reminded him that the rule of the day was cart path only. (He was only on the second hole. Had he forgotten that he was told that when he teed off?)

His reply was, "I know that, but I'm a regular."

Huh? Sad.

I guess I can be a bit sarcastic. On another very wet day, I saw a woman driving a cart right down the middle of a fairway. The cart path crosses the fairway in front of the green. I stopped on the cart path in the middle of the fairway and waited for her to approach me. She was an Asian lady. I did not say anything; I just sat there waiting for her. It was obvious that she knew she was doing something wrong.

She got out of her cart, put her hands together in a praying position, bowed, and said, "I am so sorry."

I got out of my cart, repeated her gesture, bowed, and said, "So am I, and if you don't stay on the cart path, I will take your cart keys from you, and you will walk."

We gappers were scheduled to work two or three days a week and only half a day. We were only paid minimum wage. But with the perks, it was a way to keep busy and make a little money. The men I worked with were all retired; all of them had been managers for the companies they worked for, so we were all Type A personalities.

For two years, I worked on Monday evenings. There were three industrial leagues that played at the same time on Monday night. These were all good guys and always policed themselves on the course. There were never any problems with them. But on one occasion, one of them got hurt, pretty badly too. He was in the rough on the first hole, and when he hit his ball back onto the fairway, it hit a tree, bounced back at him, and hit him in the forehead. It split his head open, and he was taken to the hospital. This was certainly not funny, until I learned he was the safety inspector for their company. When he went to work the next day, his golfing buddies had posted targets all over his office. Tough crowd.

Accidents do happen on the golf course, and the rangers have to be prepared for anything. We have to know CPR and be familiar with the first aid kits that are on all the ranger carts.

On Tuesday mornings, there were leagues for senior men and women. The men's league was fairly large. Half would tee off on the front nine, and half on the back. They only played nine holes. Some of them were pretty old and played pretty slow. There was a twenty-minute gap after they were all on the course and the senior women started. They were always anxious to begin, but we starters were told to not let them go until the twenty minutes were up because they always played faster than the men and would be on the guys' backs in no time and then complain about the slow play. If they would just be patient and wait the twenty minutes they were not likely to catch the last group of men.

I was the starter on the back nine, and after everyone was on the course, I would move over to the front and sit next to the water hazard on the par five fourth hole. It looked directly into the sun. With dew on the grass and looking into the sun, it was hard to spot your shot, so I helped the ladies find their balls. One morning, there was a dead raccoon in the right tree line as you approached the first landing area. Every group of ladies told me about the dead raccoon. The next week, all the ladies asked what happened to the raccoon. I told each of them that he was very good with mustard.

One morning, sadly, one of the senior men had a heart attack and died. Another time, a large group of Northwest Community Hospital workers were playing in an outing. One of the nurses got hit in the head by another golfer who was warming up his swing. She was taken to the hospital, was given a number of stitches, and came back to the course, finisher her round, went to the bar later, and celebrated with a beer. Tough girl.

Probably the funniest thing that happened to me was on a Saturday afternoon. This story has quite a build-up; sorry about that.

There was a group that came to play once or twice a season; they were very well known to everyone who worked at the course. They would come into the pro shop and get the counter person busy, and the others would shoplift whatever they could. They did the same thing with the beverage cart girls while they were playing. It was so bad that the gappers were alerted to this so we could protect the girls who drove the beverage carts them. One day, a member of their group came early. He asked the starter if we had a driving range so he could warm up. The starter did not recognize him as a member part of this infamous group. He informed him that yes we had a driving range, but it's in another location. The course was not busy at the time so the starter, being a nice guy, offered to let him play the first and ninth holes, which parallel each other. The ninth would bring him right back to the clubhouse.

Well, he played the first hole and then crossed the street to play number two, which is out of sight from the starter. I was called to send him back. I found him halfway down the second hole. I drove over to him and informed him, nicely, that he was only being allowed to play one and nine. He replied that I was wrong; the starter told him he could play the first few holes. I showed him my walkie-talkie and said we talked to each other, and I knew what he was allowed to do. So, are you ready for this? He offered to kick my ass.

When I told my supervisor what happened, he told me I should have removed him from the course. I said I would have, but I was laughing too hard. I told my boss that I said to him, "Well, two things: One, that isn't going to happen. And two, you're going back." I did send him back to the clubhouse.

Golf carts are pretty easy to drive. At least you'd think so. Liquor and golf are two things that should not go together, but they usually do. We had some driven into ponds. We had one driven through a fence in the driveway in front of the clubhouse. I stopped one girl from driving hers onto a green. She stopped literally inches from the surface of the green.

One lady, who was playing in an outing, stopped me and said she lost her jacket. She asked me to see if I could locate it for her. Players are always leaving a club somewhere, and we were often asked to locate them. This was the first time I was asked to find a jacket. I literally drove the entire couse looking and asking about her jacket. It was in her car.

The Monday evening industrial leagues were always fun. The Tuesday senior men and women's leagues were always fun. The Saturday morning regular groups were always fun. Saturday afternoons and evenings, open to the public hackers, not so much.

I did a lot of things in my work life, but I never dealt with the public. This was a real education. I finally retired. I finally decided to finish this stupid book.

So my mom was right: I did teach school, and I became a salesman. I had some good times, some not-so-good times. I did try to enjoy myself, because as Dad told me, whatever you do for a third of your life, you should enjoy it. As you can see, I did a bunch of things over my work years to support myself and my family. I have been very lucky. I have a wonderful, incredibly supportive wife, two wonderful daughters who have good husbands, and they have given us six delightful grandchildren. If I can give the reader any advice, it would be this:

As Dad said, 'Life is too short to not have fun living it." Be kind to others; be honest with yourself and others. As my first boss told me, never ever lie. It is easy to forget lies, but you can always remember the truth, even if it hurts. He also said to handle a piece of paper correctly the first time, and it won't come back to haunt you. Whenever you can, nice to everyone, but don't take any crap. Life is too short not to have some fun and enjoy it.

Printed in the United States
by Baker & Taylor Publisher Services